TEN P'S IN A POD

TEN P'S IN A POD
A Million-Mile Journal *of the* Arnold Pent Family

Arnold Pent III

THE VISION FORUM, INC.
SAN ANTONIO, TEXAS

"Where there is no vision, the people perish."

The Vision Forum, Inc.
4719 Blanco Rd., San Antonio, Texas 78212
1-800-440-0022
www.visionforum.com

ISBN 1-929241-89-5

Illustrations by Peter Pent

Typesetting and Cover Design by
Shannon G. Moeller

PRINTED IN THE UNITED STATES OF AMERICA

Dedicated to my Father and Mother
who caused all of this

Contents

About the Author

Arnold Van Dyke Pent, Sr., cigar manufacturer of Philadelphia, was converted to Christ at the age of forty-five and sold his business, being ordained to the Gospel ministry after graduating from Bible school. In the meantime, he sent his son, Arnold V. Pent, Jr., to Wheaton Academy and Wheaton College in 1917, who after graduation, entered the Bible Institute of Pennsylvania (now the Philadelphia College of Bible and Graduate School), graduating in 1925; being at that time also ordained to the Ministry. After marrying Persis Eames in 1935, the Lord gave them the eight children that became the offspring of this story. The third offspring and second son, Arnold Pent III, wrote this book from his diary between the ages of seventeen and nineteen.

Foreword

A Million Miles of Family Discipleship
Beall Phillips

Our family travels quite a bit. If not Doug and one of the children, then it is all ten of us, including the very fine young man who lives with us. When all ten of us travel together, we get into some hilarious and some harrowing situations. We've been gawked at, hooted at, pulled over, cheered on, clapped at, gaped at, and murmured about. We've been called a private school, a daycare, a circus, a zoo, and probably privately by some, a nuthouse.

We have the idiosyncrasies that go with a large and growing family: We march in a line, according to age, to keep order. We often wear matching clothes so no one gets lost, or, if someone does, they are easily identified and returned. We love to be together, work together, play together. We love to travel together, and all the stares make us smile inside and out, because we just love our big family.

So, when the children and I first read *Ten P's in a Pod*, we laughed and snorted and sighed and cried. The Arnold Pent family is what our family would have looked like if we had lived in the '40s and '50s. The father knows exactly what he wants done and how. The mother's goal is to make it happen and keep everybody happy in the process. The children, eager and youthful, are an integral part of the father's vision and provide bucket-loads of humor. Together, they make up what has been called "The World's Most Unusual Family."

Before seatbelt laws and car seats, before the suburban fad and the rise of the fifteen-passenger van, the ten-person Pent family was driving an interesting collection of automobiles one million miles around and around and around the country, preaching about the saving love of Jesus and the importance of the Bible in daily life. Before my generation rediscovered that real butter is better than margarine, that whole grain breads are better than white fluff, and that exercise must be vigorous and constant, the Pent family knew and practiced all of this. Thirty years before the explosion of home schooling in the early '80s, the Pents were home schooling their children because, "I just don't think it's right to let an atheist or non-believer have our children the best part of every day teaching them many things that we will have to turn right around and tell them are not true."

Ten P's in a Pod was first published two years before I was born. Most of the Pent children were adults before I could put a sentence together. But I relate to and understand their experiences and their story as if it were my own. This is a slice of life. This is the day-to-day in a not-so-average American Christian family. Everyone who reads this book will feel the same way and relate to one part or another. But reading *Ten P's in a Pod* is not even like reading! It is really like having a conversation with the author, Arnold, third of the eight children, about his family, their life experiences as they traveled, and their passion for the gospel of Jesus Christ. It is simple, it is profound, and it is a riot!

Beyond the humor and crazy scrapes that we all get ourselves into is the ultimately important message of the book: work together as a family and make the Word of God an integral part of your daily life. It sounds so simple, and yet, you will walk away from this story fundamentally inspired and motivated.

The Original, All-American Home School Family Band
Doug Phillips

Future historians may look back on the Arnold Pent family and describe them as the "first modern home school family." Long before there were any state home schooling organizations, curriculum fairs, and before the very term "home education" was in vogue, Arnold Pent declared his independence from government education and his dependence on Jesus Christ in the training of his children.

No one told him to do this. He simply read the Bible and determined to follow the clear principles found within its pages. He determined to be obedient to God regardless of the consequences from truant officers, school superintendents, or even well-intentioned Christians who could not understand why any father would want to spend so much time with his family.

Of course, Arnold Pent did not invent home education. Parent-directed education is as old as the earth, but the modern home school movement was birthed out of a self-conscious desire on the part of parents to do three things: (1) to go back to the biblical roots of education and discipleship; (2) to build family unity through shared vision, ministry, and a family-friendly lifestyle; and (3) to turn their hearts to their children and to pray that God would turn the hearts of their children to them. Upon these three principles, the Pent family embarked upon one of the great family journeys of the 1950s. It was a journey of faith that brought them a million miles in their automobiles, that equipped them to memorize much of the Bible by heart, and that knit the hearts of the children in this family one to another such that they remain constant in their love and devotion nearly fifty years later.

Like all great visionary leaders, Arnold Pent was a man with many glorious and wonderful directives for his family. The world would probably describe these initiatives as eccentricities or idiosyncrasies, but they were neither. They were the stuff of which true leadership is made. In fact, Arnold Pent discovered something that all fathers would be well advised to consider: True Christian leadership in the household is born in the fire of adversity. The noblest and most God-blessed expressions of biblical fatherhood are cultivated always and only by taking the path less traveled.

I feel a special kinship to the Pent family. As a boy, I traveled constantly with my father. By the time I was eighteen, I had been to forty-nine of the fifty states with my father. I sat with him for tens of thousands of miles and listened to books on tape, sermons, histories, and theology lectures. They were glorious, glorious times. We discussed everything. We saw great sites. There were moments of great humor and moments of tremendous difficulty. But I always felt like I was a part of my father's life mission. There is no doubt in my mind that my life was shaped and formed by a father who made it his commitment to have me by his side and to daily speak words of life and love into my heart.

As Beall and I seek to raise our own children in the

fear and admonition of the Lord, I daily think back to the
example established for me by my father. I desire with all
my heart to be for my children what my father was for me.
Ten P's in a Pod has not only filled our house with laughter,
but it has reminded me of the mission that God has set
before my bride and me. For this, I am truly grateful.

Over the years, many readers have been attracted to
the endearing stories of family life found in such classics
as Kathryn Forbes' *Mamma's Bank Account* (also called
I Remember Mamma), Clarence Day's *Life with Father*,
and the turn of the century classic by Frank Gilbreth,
Cheaper by the Dozen. The beauty of the book in your
hands is that it combines the very best elements of family
humor embodied in those classics with a distinctive
and uncompromising Gospel message. As a publisher,
I consider it the highest honor that the Lord and His
servants, the Pent family, have allowed Vision Forum to
bring to press what we believe will be a new classic for
twenty-first century families.

Doug and Beall Phillips
Grateful Christian Parents to Seven Children

Introduction

Dad and Ma were something like circuit ridin' preachers who bought the largest horseless carriage available and brought us along as object lessons and illustrations...every time.

They absolutely needed big cars because their little "object lessons" were increasing every year and all us little "lessons" made pretty crabby "objects" if we didn't have a seat to sit on.

As if it weren't enough to own the biggest thing on wheels and more children than the lady in the shoe, they deemed it wise to purchase such vintage transportation as the Pierce Arrow and Packard and traveled nearly a million miles before some of us realized the world was round.

Eight of us, along with Father and Mother makes a grand total of ten Pents, and with that many of anything in one car, boat or buggy, there's bound to be action both positive and negative. But just as in photography it takes a good negative to produce a good picture, so it is in our Christian lives. Remember, if we don't have any battles, we won't have any victories. And the Apostle Paul tells us in First Timothy, "Fight the good fight of faith, lay hold on eternal life, whereunto thou art also called..."

A million miles might not sound like a whole lot in

1

this day of jets and missiles, but when you have taken a good share of that in Packard and Pierce Arrow cars on puddle and piece-meal roads packed in with nine other "P's" in a "Pod" like ours put together back in the 1930's, you begin to ponder whether that was five million miles instead of just one million.

But God has given our family an important purpose in all this traveling, and as we follow His plan for our lives, we sure enjoy life on the puddle and piece-meal roads. We are thankful for every mile.

Now that I have reached that ripe old age of twenty-one and have a million miles behind me, I am realizing that things just don't last forever. Neither cars nor trucks nor airplanes are eternal and they wear out and go to pieces. Only what is done for the Lord will last forever.

I will always remember one of Father's frequently quoted verses from James 4:14-15. Addressing all eight of us "en masse" with his booming voice and penetrating every fiber of our being, he would quote: "For what is your life? It is even a vapor, that appeareth for a little time, and then vanisheth away. For that ye ought to say, If the Lord will, we shall live, and do this, or that."

This perspective on life, along with the habit of reading the Scripture daily as a family was the most valuable heritage they possibly could have given us.

Ten P's in a Pod is the story of our life up to this time in 1965. We could never have planned out the adventures God has taken us on. Proverbs 20:24 says, "Man's goings are of the Lord; how can a man then understand his own way?" and Proverbs 16:9 says, "A man's heart deviseth his way: but the Lord directeth his steps." As we have followed His direction, we've had a great time, learned to love Him and to love each other.

We cannot guess what lies before us, or what part of the world our travels will take us to next. We just trust the Lord with all our heart and do not lean on our own understanding. We are committed to acknowledging Him in all our ways and know that he will make our path straight. (Proverbs 3:5-6)

1

First-Class Comfort

We were now in Pensacola, Florida getting a little rest, after working hard the year previous. We rented a house on the beach and just rested—that is, it was rest to us. Some people might not call selling fertilizer from early morning till late at night a rest, but in this case we did. This was a different kind of work, therefore it was rest for us, because we had been holding meetings in churches, schools, clubs, plus appearances on T.V. and radio programs for the past year.

Believe me, it's a lot easier for ten people to work at the job of spreading fertilizer and planting nursery stock than it is for ten people to travel around the country living in motels, people's houses, cars, and trailers, not to mention the different types of people you meet with different ideas, different backgrounds, and different temperaments. They try to tell you their life story, propound their unfounded theories on religion, and last but by far not the least, they eye you every minute in order to be able to compose— what they consider—a very profound stereotype of you, which contains all your good, bad, and indifferent habits.

During this brief period we rested harder than we'd rested for ages. Every morning we got up early and "rested" like a "dog" mixing fertilizer. Then we would go out and "rest" like a "Trojan" spreading fertilizer on people's lawns.

That wasn't always our privilege while we were traveling. Ironically enough, one night it was a nice bed with a Beautyrest mattress, and the next night it was a creaky army cot with one broken leg, down in somebody's cellar.

Here's a trip from Pensacola, Florida to Schenectady, New York, where we had been invited to bring the whole family and present the many songs we had learned at family devotions and dramatize the Bible stories we have become so familiar with.

On this seven hundred mile trip, time and providence had given us only one little Ford panel truck to transport us and all our luggage and instruments to the desired destination.

The number one item on the agenda early Monday morning to prepare for the trip was not packing, map reading, or house cleaning, but Bible reading.

From Charlotte—the youngest—right up to Dad, everybody found a quiet nook in the house, in the truck, or out on the beach nearby getting in private Bible reading and prayer, which is routine no matter where we go (15-30 minutes for the younger ones and one hour for the older ones).

After devotions, each one pursued his own exercising plan, ranging from blond-haired Timothy (5 years old) getting in his one sit-up and one-half push-up, to Paul and me with sixty sit-ups and fifty push-ups.

After breakfast came our time of family devotions reading the Bible, singing in harmony, and asking God's guidance for the day's task. Incidentally, we try to "Let the word of Christ dwell in us richly." That's why in our family circle each one reads a chapter or two instead of a verse or two.

As the last "Amen" of family devotions was sounded, Dad, in order to leave on schedule, started orders flying in every direction. "Arnold and Paul, you get the truck fixed

6

up to accommodate eight people. We've decided, being so short on room, to let Ma and Charlotte take the train up to see grandma and we'll pick them up in Boston later. Pete and Tim, you fellows get all the baggage to the back of the truck; Dave help them with heavy items and hang all the best clothes on wire across the back. Connie, Liz, and Char, help Ma get everything cleaned up and let's be out of here in forty minutes."

Since this was the first any of us had been informed of taking a trip, the scene from then on made Grand Central Station look like Sleeping Beauty, and it seemed

like just a couple of minutes later when that familiar voice of authority rang down the hallways, "You kids get that truck loaded, we've got a long trip ahead and anything or anybody that's not in there in twenty minutes gets left."

As it turned out, that last twenty minutes barely gave Paul and me time to get everything in, much less getting it packed anywhere near the state of neatness, not even to mention undertaking a seating arrangement for the whole crowd in that small panel truck. So when the zero hour came, Dad was at the wheel with a determined look on his face tooting the horn, and we had to grab everything left in sight and crawl through the back door, draping ourselves the best we could over the mountains of boxes and clothes and instruments in the back of the truck.

Gradually as we hit a few bumps on the way out of town, the luggage proceeded to settle and we began to seep down into the load like cheese melting over an open fire.

I finally landed right side up on Connie's big black suitcase and propped my feet on the Kellogg's Corn Flake box packed with all our sheets and towels as the truck turned North.

Dad, Elisabeth, Connie, and Peter were in the front seat. That is, Dad had the seat. Connie was sitting on a milk crate we picked up in California, and Elisabeth was firmly planted into some pillows with Peter stuffed between the cracks.

Paul was sitting in the back on an old car seat hastily maneuvered into position, not noticing the handles of two fertilizer shovels near at hand to jab him in the ribs if Dad applied the brakes with any fervor. They were ready to jab him because I was leaning against the other end of the shovels for a backrest, and when the truck lurched, I lurched. David had Timothy on his lap and was sitting on the other end of the seat which Paul and the shovel handles were occupying but was not paying particular attention to the big box just behind him piled high above his head with pots and pans, arranged like tossed salad in a wringer washing machine, and ready to descend upon him at the slightest provocation.

I don't remember much between my landing ceremony on the suitcase and sometime later, but suddenly, Dad's foot hit the power brakes like a falling meteor and four simultaneous squeals ascended to the skies amidst the

flying debris. There was one from me, slammed against the shovel blades, with an immediate response from behind where Paul received the rounded ends of the shovels in his rib cage. One from Peter, who nearly hit the ceiling with a splinter in his thigh, and one from David who by now was lifting the pressure cooker off his ears.

Time was fast running out and the deadline in Schenectady was drawing nearer, so we all voted to eat as we drove. Connie and Liz purchased some groceries passing through a small town and brought them on board. I can remember at least four quarts of milk, two loaves of bread, a jar of mayonnaise, a head of lettuce, cheese and cookies, and that we were all terribly hungry after bouncing around all morning over twisting country roads. We knew it wasn't going to be an easy job to get that in our hungry frames so everybody cooperated to get it in eatable shape.

I was elected to make the sandwiches, since I was sitting on the only flat surface to be found—Connie's big black suitcase. I laid out the food and started to mayonnaise the bread with one of our family advertising leaflets while David broke the cheese into eight equal chunks. He then handed each piece, via Paul, back to my assembly plant where they were joined with a few succulent lettuce chunks and the bread and mayonnaise. They were all finally made and each one received his custom-made hors d' oeuvre.

Then Dad spoke up, and above the general commotion, said, "Let's all bow our heads and thank the Lord for the food and His faithfulness in supplying it to us three times every day." So we all bowed our heads as Dad thanked the Lord for "filling our hearts with food and gladness and supplying our every need." As I think back now, it was really a simple prayer but packed with Dad's ever-present optimism, and in a way seemed to encompass all we stood for; simply one family following the Lord and His Word day by day and determining to follow His commission to "Go ye into all the world and preach the Gospel to every creature."

As the meal got under way, there was the question of drinking those four quarts of milk as we bounced around among the luggage. I had taken eight paper cups from the last service station where we filled up with gas, and now drew them out of my back pocket. Except for the fact that they were perfectly flattened, everything else about them was normal and each one re-shaped it as he saw fit.

Paul spoke up and said, "I think we should all pour our own milk over our own lap. In that way it won't be anybody's fault but his own if he gets more on his lap than he does in his cup." The vote was unanimous and Paul took the lead, "pouring his own milk over his own lap" and demonstrating the model method.

Paul was the first one to take a milk bath. Then Connie leaned over from the front seat. "Honestly, Paul, is that the best you can do? Here, let me show you." So the half-gallon container was handed up to the front seat

where Connie gingerly poured—Connie was the second to one to take a milk bath. It was that way for about the first two quarts until we all learned the art of swinging ourselves, the cup, and milk along with the swing of the truck, the seat, and the road.

After much struggling and these practice shots, we all got some milk and started to drink. Just then Dad hit the shoulder of the road and we all felt the milk speeding past our Adams apple down to our stomachs, the only difficulty was, it went via the chin and not the throat.

By now most of the milk was either somewhere in the luggage or on the floor leaking through the cracks to the road, so we decided to give the whole episode up for a bad job and everybody settled back for our regular family devotions which would all have to be quoted since reading was impossible on these rough roads.

Dad started out by quoting Psalm one, followed by Liz on Psalm two, Peter on Psalm three and right along the line, all the way back to me finishing the first round on Psalm eight.

Then Dad started in quoting the eighth chapter of Romans: "There is therefore now no condemnation to them which are in Christ Jesus, who walk not after the flesh, but after the Spirit," and when he had finished the chapter, I decided to follow with Romans nine, "I say the truth in Christ, I lie not, my conscience also bearing me witness in the Holy Ghost, that I have great heaviness and continual sorrow in my heart." Dave was next in line and I guess he reasoned the next thing on schedule was Romans ten, so he started in, "Brethren, my hearts desire and prayer to God for Israel is, that they might be saved." Paul didn't disappoint anybody either because he came right out quoting the eleventh chapter, " I say then, hath God cast away his people? God forbid." And Connie wrapped up the whole session very appropriately by giving none other than Romans twelve, "I beseech you therefore, brethren, by the mercies of God, that ye present your bodies a living sacrifice, holy, acceptable unto God, which is your reasonable service."

After that twenty-five minutes of quoting, we all sang together and each one prayed. (The many chapters and books of the Bible we are now able to quote without trying to memorize is the direct result of these thirty minutes of family devotions after every meal. My father and mother believe that when the Bible says, "Thou shalt teach these things diligently to thy children," it means just that!)

As evening came on, we were still six hours driving time from Schenectady, and as it started snowing, Dad, talking half to himself and half to us said, "We'll never make it to Schenectady tonight, so we'll keep our eye open for a reasonably priced motel." Then pulling his wallet from his back pocket, said, "Connie, count up our total assets and see how our money is holding out." It didn't take her long because thirty seconds later she reported that there were only fifteen dollars left. "There's one thing sure," said Dad, taking a deep breath, "we can't stay in a motel, and eat, and buy gas and get to Schenectady all on fifteen dollars. Does anybody have any money they would like to put in the general fund? If so, give it to Connie and we'll take a tally. Remember, this is the Lord's work and He tells us in Matthew, 'Lay up for yourselves treasures in heaven, where neither moth nor rust doth corrupt, and where thieves do not break through nor steal.'"

All of a sudden, a silent hush fell upon each of us as we thoughtfully and painfully poured our spending plans down the drain. (Of course, this wasn't the first time it had happened, but some days when this was asked of us and our travel-beaten vision of life could only measure security in dollars and cents, living took on a despairing mood. That is, until we actually trusted God for our little world and by faith, small though it was, gave for the spread of the Good News. Giving was a little easier each time and we began to realize that from these little sacrifices and personal experiences, God was revealing His wisdom to us and that truly, "the merchandise of it is better than the merchandise of silver, and the gain thereof than fine gold.")

Then slowly and methodically there was a stirring as we all dug our small savings from handkerchiefs, suitcase, or pockets and emptied them into the general fund.

We arrived in Schenectady the next day in good time for the meetings we had looked forward to, prayed for, and struggled to reach.

As we sang of the mercies of the Lord, dramatized Bible stories, and explained how we had trusted Jesus Christ as our personal Lord and Savior, we saw children and teenagers, young people and adults believe on the Lord Jesus Christ, saved from the "wages of sin" which is death, and receive the "gift of God which is eternal life through Jesus Christ our Lord."

My excitement grew as I stood and watched the people all around me confess publicly that they too would trust Jesus as their Savior, as the Holy Spirit used the Word of God I had helped to give. What a thrill that God would let me share His glories and reap eternal rewards. Paul must have felt it when he explained in Ephesians one, "That ye may know what is the hope of his calling, and what the riches of the glory of his inheritance in the saints, and what is the exceeding greatness of his power toward us who believe."

Why, that bumpy truck ride wasn't so bad after all, and those meals? Well, they could have been a lot worse, and what was a little money? It was worth everything to be able to stand up to an audience and say with confidence and conviction, "If any man be in Christ, he is a new creation, old things are passed away, behold all things are become new."

When God gives me a family, I might not buy Pierce Arrow cars and have more children than the lady in the shoe, and travel a million miles—and then again, I might—but I will pass on to those I love, the priceless heritage of Bible reading and prayer and opportunities to serve the Lord together.

After a profitable week in Schenectady, we started to load up to go to Boston. (Being in one place that long required considerable luggage carrying from the upstairs apartment where we had stayed.)

The first package for loading came down with Elisabeth who was daintily tiptoeing with her expensive luggage carrier to the back of the truck. You have no idea how utterly costly this piece of equipment was. It was a "Farm Fresh" egg box that had seen more states than most business executives. Next came eight-year-old Peter with all his worldly possessions in a little Boston bag, with five-year-old Timothy close at his heels with similar gear.

The truck was finally loaded with—it seemed—twice as much as we arrived with. Without fail it always happened that way, either things were given to us or we didn't have the time it takes (at least an hour) to pack everything scientifically the way it should be packed if we were going to be comfortable. After many friendly goodbyes we rolled out of Schenectady, New York, and headed for Boston.

The first thing we did after we got away from the crowds was to thank the God whom we serve for the wonderful response we had received from people there, and for the fact that many of them promised that they would be diligent to read the Bible daily. This is one of our main objectives; that people wake up to the fact that unless they find God and Faith through the Bible, they've missed the main purpose of living, because the Bible itself says, "Let us hear the conclusion of the whole matter: Fear God, and keep his commandments: for this is the whole duty of man. For God shall bring every work into judgment, with every secret thing, whether it be good, or whether it be evil."

We knew from our million miles of travel and personal experience that whether you are rich, medium, or poor, even though many of us find it inconvenient to our ego to obey God and do what he tells us to do, yet we have a certain craving for peace with ourselves, our families, and the Lord, and it only comes when we yield our lives completely to Him. If only we would crucify our pride and come to Him, we could realize the thrill and reality and promise He gave before He was crucified, "Peace I leave with you, my peace I give unto you: not as the world giveth, give I unto you. Let not your heart be troubled, neither let it be afraid," and then put into practice the Apostle Paul's statement, "I am crucified with Christ; nevertheless I live; yet not I, but Christ liveth in me: and the life which I now live in the flesh I live by faith of the Son of God, who loved me, and gave himself for me."

2

Canadian Customs

The continuation of our travels brought us into Northern New Hampshire where we saw God working for us in a wonderful way. We went up to a small town on the border between New Hampshire and Quebec, Canada, not knowing what to expect because we had nothing arranged, nor did we know anyone.

We rented two cabins just outside of Littleton, New Hampshire and since Father had registered his plant food and received a license as he drove through Concord, the state capitol, he announced the next morning that the male population of the family was going to go sell fertilizer door to door and make some money to pay expenses.

One of the first prospects Father went to see was the largest hotel in the whole White Mountain area in view of beautiful Mt. Washington. It is an exclusive hotel that boasts of swimming pools and a golf course and many luxuries.

One of the providences I was impressed with while growing up at this time was the unusual favor and trust Father received from total strangers. As he went in to see a prospective customer for his fertilizer, never could he say, "I'm from 219 Main St." or "just off Broadway," or "Mr. Jones said he told you about our product;" and yet without these advantages and the asset of a large company behind

17

him, he could sell this stuff like popcorn at the county fair.

Of course many times in the urgent conditions he found himself with the responsibility of caring for a wife, eight children, and deadlines to meet, he would talk a prospect deaf, dumb, and blind until they bought out of self-defense. However, most of the time without undue pressure, the sales would be good. My personal opinion is that God was honoring his faith and courage when many others would do nothing but sit around and criticize. God promises, "Them that honor me, I will honor." (1 Samuel 2:30) and, "The wicked are overthrown, and are not: but the house of the righteous shall stand." (Proverbs 12:7) Anyway, Father went in to see the buyer for the hotel and after forty-five minutes, he descended from the main entrance whistling triumphantly. Success is one thing Dad can never hide. I can always tell a mile away whether he makes a sale just by the way he walks.

The story here was they wanted us to fertilize all the golf greens but on the basis that when the saw the results they would pay. This wasn't the ultimate in arrangements, cash is always more attractive, but the deal was clinched and the job done.

On Wednesday night since no meeting had been arranged anywhere, everybody got in the cars, (Father had replaced the truck with a battery of three old cars bought at a bargain), and we drove into the small town of Littleton, New Hampshire to look for a place to go to prayer meeting. The first church we saw was the one right on the square in the center of town.

Father walked into the large, typically New England stone edifice and found the spiritual life there was colder than the stones that surrounded it. All he found were two elderly ladies over in the corner praying.

After a little pep talk on what we were doing, Father had generated so much enthusiasm into these two, they decided to go ask the small prayer group from a church right behind theirs to come over and listen too.

In a few minutes these valiant ladies that had not known five minutes ago that we existed came walking through the church doors with a couple of dozen curious people from the church next door. (Incidentally, the beliefs of these two churches were worlds apart and helped make this even more interesting.)

I don't remember exactly how the meeting went, but I do remember the results at the close. Many of those who heard us trusted Christ as Savior and there was a real revival of praying in both churches.

From the unusual meeting that night we were invited to present a program to the town's 350 teenagers at the local high school the very next day and conducted a special service in the Congregational Church that Sunday.

When the neighboring town heard what was going on they invited us for a combined service with their two churches for Sunday morning, and packed out the town hall Sunday night.

The results were astonishing with many of the high school students trusting Christ and courageously making their faith and belief known throughout the whole area. People that had never seen the inside of a church and were completely ignorant of God's mercy or justice were sitting in the services and repenting of their sin.

Most of these people were hard working farmers and didn't have much money to give, but the Lord so blessed the sale of our plant food and honored each one's faith and work, there was enough to pay all expenses and a little to start into Canada.

So, we drove across the Canadian border with these old cars, a family of ten, no definite schedule arranged, and a grand sum of nine dollars in our collective pockets.

Father's official statement was very simple: "All I know is the Lord told us to go up and preach and that's what we're going to do."

When we stopped at Canadian Customs for a routine inspection, the man eyed us curiously. Of course, anything connected with us doesn't usually turn out to be very routine, but the inspector didn't know this yet.

To begin with, he did look slightly bewildered at our presence there, but why shouldn't he, faced with this caravan? Peter, Timothy, and Charlotte displayed their travel smudged faces in innocent grandeur from the car windows to get a look at the inspector, while he tried to look in and see what in the world we were carrying.

First he looked in the 1950 Packard that was full of Daddy, Mamma, Elisabeth, and Charlotte. The back deck was unarranged strictly family style, complete with coats,

20

school books, and all sorts of indescribable material. Then
the inevitable happened! He wanted to see what was in the
back trunk. We all shrank in horror as it was opened. I'm
sure the man must have thought we fell off a garbage truck
or something, because the trunk was full of our empty, beat
up fertilizer boxes and bags left over from the business in
New Hampshire.

Then he said with all the authority he could muster,
"What's this?" "Well, ah, they're fertilizer boxes, sir," my
father answered. "Well," he said, "what are you doing
with fertilizer boxes?" Then my father really let go with
all the masterful oratorical experience he could remember
and told the dear old inspector that we were raised in the
nursery business and we were just helping nurse some
plants and lawns back to health in New Hampshire, and
we hadn't had time to get rid of the boxes yet.

Well, down with the back trunk of the Packard and
off to the Buick. Believe me folks; this 1950 Buick was a
dooser! When you drove from a red light, it knocked like a
woodpecker, and gave off so much smoke you'd almost think
it was an old-fashioned freight train. Up walked the inspector
who took a peek inside. The car looked like a traveling
junkyard because we had all our best clothes hanging up in
the back plus our best, "Samsonite cardboard Campbell's
tomato soup can boxes," which contained our Swiss cheese
type undershirts, etc., plus our pants and double entry
socks—you know, the kind you can enter through the top and
exit through the heel, or the toe, or both.

The inspector walked up and, well, he sorta sighed and
didn't even try to open the back doors.

After looking in the window and seeing nothing but
a cardboard box smashed against it, he walked around to
the back trunk. The back trunk he was now looking at had

been quilted by a dirt truck, and in the process lost the lock. Therefore, it was tied to the bumper with that stuff that usually runs around the inside edge of the car door to keep the wind out. Well, thank the Lord he didn't try to open it because it was tied awful tight and if once he'd gotten it open, it would have been filled with the same stuff that he had seen in the back seat.

Then he turned to car number three. It was a somewhat more refined looking car with a conservative gray coat of paint. The 1951 Desoto was carrying a neat load of pots, pans, pillows, and all sorts of household necessities, which Ma had decided to bring along. He asked David, Paul, and me where we were born and how old we were, gave the car a casual looking over—I suppose being somewhat exhausted from the other two nightmares—and passed us through the gate.

3

Getting Started

Being born into the traveling Pent family is a lot more exciting than most people realize. I know this for a fact because I'm on the inside looking out and every mile carries more excitement and every day carries more challenge. During the past thirty years our family has traveled over one million miles together.

Dad and Ma started out in the depression years and consequently, their first honeymoon home was built by my father's very own hands. Being a man of many talents and possessing determination to put them to good use, he decided he should build the first family residence.

It was a cozy little home; something two people could really cuddle up in, and cuddle they did, because the measurements were six feet wide and twenty feet long; and underneath its center was an axle, and on the end of each axle, a tire.

This mansion on wheels consisted of a single bed over each wheel well, and that's all; except an aisle between the beds.

As you might have guessed, it wasn't long before there was a crowd instead of two. The arrival of David, only the first of a much larger crowd to come, necessitated some changes in living quarters. Actually it was all very simple— just bring in another bed. This innovation made our first living quarters one big "happy" bed on wheels.

After the trailer came a square frame house with four cedar posts firmly imbedded on the Maine coastline, also built by the master of assemblies, Father Pent. This became headquarters and was used frequently between our travels.

Automobiles really went through our family in a hurry, or it might be more accurate to say, we went through them in a hurry. Anyway, one by one they would groan under the strain and just stop dead. Thirty years later, forty cars and trucks had been used right down to the last back seat.

One old-timer and the oldest car we ever owned was a 1932 Packard, and by the time we bought it, was quite out of style and very homely. The new sleek models were just coming in with shiny bright colored paint jobs and automatic gears. This big "Noah's Ark on wheels" had a huge motor with twelve cylinders, big running boards, huge round headlights that protruded like bulging eyeballs on the front fenders, and seats for everybody and his neighbor. It must have weighed at least a couple of tons and had a gas and oil bill to match all these features. Actually, mileage was about four miles to the gallon and Dad always kept those two gallon oil cans stored in the back trunk and when the men would be pumping gas into the back, he would be pouring oil into the front.

On another occasion, we owned the greatly respected Pierce Arrow car. This respect showed itself more in fear than in admiration because comparison between this, and the cars of that day were like that of a mouse and a lion. It was a mighty vehicle and people didn't get in your way. One feature made it immortal. It would never start in the mornings and always had to be parked on a hill. Many a morning, so Dad could get off to work, David, Connie, Elisabeth, and I received a message delivered by little Paul, "Daddy said to come as you are and help him get the car started." A minute or two later pajamas, nightgowns, and frazzled heads were lined up along the bumper and had to push until she coughed up the magic formula. As soon as the coughing came with rapid regularity, we knew the job was done and nothing could stop her now. By the time we caught our breath, Dad was almost out of sight. Not necessarily because he was far away, but the cloud of dust and exhaust rather obscured our vision.

One autumn as we were driving from Maine to Florida, we thought this car had given its last mile. We had been traveling all day at the death-defying speed of thirty-five miles per hour and for some reason we kept pushing ahead into the night, (not traveling very speedily but at least steadily). About nine o' clock, deep in a southeastern state, the rear end of the car gave a loud, deafening grind, snapped its connections, and hit the road with a thud. Then the old chariot jerked to a stop and the stifling smell of hot steel and burnt oil put us beside ourselves with fear and we piled out into the darkness.

About the only reason we stopped was because cars just don't roll without rear ends. If it had kept rolling, we would have kept going no matter what the noise because it

was miles from any town and there wasn't a soul to help us.

Seeing that nothing could be done to fix it, we jumped the fence near the road and started walking, following the fence that followed the highway. It was so pitch black you could almost feel it, so Dad organized his frightened little flock so that we stretched out in a long row, locking arms with each other to keep from being separated and stumbling on the rough ground.

After about forty-five minutes of wearisome trudging, suddenly Ma pointed ahead and said, "Look, a light." As hope was rekindled with sight of civilization, our pace quickened and sure enough, ten minutes later we discerned a filling station.

In another five minutes, a man calmly eating a sandwich and drinking a cup of coffee had his filling station humming with strange voices that came out of nowhere, and he appeared at the door with big bewildering question marks in both brown eyes.

After Dad explained our situation to him, he got on the telephone and tried to explain what we had and what we needed. Finally, something that had the similarity of a wrecker drove into the station and even though our car was almost as big as the wrecker and moving it proved to be quite an assignment, the man managed getting us all into town.

As it turned out, the repair job was sixty dollars, and it all but cleaned us out of earthly treasures. Nevertheless, two day later that big old Pierce Arrow rolled over the Florida line, defying all handicaps and impossibilities.

Of course, the God we serve is the one who controls the circumstances, possible or impossible, and this was one more time He had seen us through safe and sound.

A verse from Isaiah (45:2,3) that gave us a lot of courage at that time says, "I will go before thee, and make the crooked places straight: I will break in pieces the gates of brass, and cut in sunder the bars of iron: And I will give thee the treasures of darkness, and hidden riches of secret places, that thou mayest know that I, the Lord, which call thee by thy name, am the God of Israel."

Many times God uses the combination of men and their money, but often and with more glory and pleasure, He uses the combination of just men and their Almighty God. He wants men to trust Him completely for their welfare. Once this is learned and practiced, things go much more smoothly. If the Lord wants to use us without money and we are trusting Him completely, the nervous tension and fear has no room to enter. If the Lord sees fit to use us with money, sometimes He supplies it miraculously, and other times He gives us the ingenuity to earn it.

In our experiences traveling, we have had both types of supply lines and it makes life very interesting.

One time when we were traveling south during the early days of our family, my father did not have the twenty-five cent toll to get across the Hudson River on the New York Ferry. This was during the Depression years and very few had any money to speak of, and you had to have more than a thimbleful of brains to earn your living. Here we were at the Hudson River and the only way across was via the ferry and twenty-five cents toll.

My father had experience in the nursery business and selling evergreen trees and conceived the following idea: He walked into the woods above the ferry and carefully dug three New England birch trees, just large enough to fit into three paper cups; then driving to a residential district he went from door to door selling New England birch trees at three for a quarter. As he knocked at the first door with his right hand and held the birch trees in his left, a

well-dressed lady appeared and Dad told her about "today's special." It just so happened she had been wanting some birch trees and the transaction was completed very quickly. Then driving back to the ferry he gave the toll-keeper the quarter and proceeded on his way.

This is an example of God giving the ingenuity to earn the money, which is one type of supply line He uses. God tells all those that love Him, "I will give you a mouth and wisdom, which all your adversaries shall not be able to gainsay nor resist." Luke 21:15

The wonder-working, providential part of God's program in keeping His men and supplies moving is the most fascinating part of my Christian experience. The following incidents will show you why.

During these early years of our family, we worked in Florida doing pioneer work and helping in an effort to start churches and establish a winter Bible Conference. Since winter Bible Conferences were a new idea and churches were never easy to start, our support from sympathetic people was very rare in word and in deed.

Just when we were at the lowest spot in the barrel, something happened that gave our faith a real boost upward. The whole thing came about (through God's direction, of course) because my father had been an athlete in college and knew the benefits of regular exercise, and because my mother enjoyed taking long walks.

One day as they were both out walking and wondering where the next meal was coming from, something directed Mother's eyes on the ground where she saw an old crumpled piece of brown paper. For some reason she picked it up, unraveled it, and lo and behold, it was an old rain-washed, sun bleached ten-dollar bill. The bank gladly exchanged it and they gladly spent it.

Another incident involving a ten-dollar bill occurred in New York.

After presenting our programs of music and Scripture drama to youth groups, we had only two dollars to make a five hundred mile destination the next day. It so happened that all the places where we worked in New York wanted to mail their contributions to us at a later date and for one reason or another, we only had two dollars.

Early the next morning, we headed out of town with two dollars to go five hundred miles. Just as we were getting out of town and on the right highway, Dad turned around in his seat, looked us all over with contented admiration, and then with confidence beaming all over his face said, "Late last night a lady came to our hostess who had never met us, heard us, or seen us and told her to be sure the Pent family got this ten dollars. She said she had heard we were doing a good work and something was telling her to make sure we got it before we left." Suffice it to say, we reached the five hundred mile destination with two dollars to spare, and enough faith to go a thousand more.

A year later that "two dollars to one thousand mile ratio in faith" helped us tremendously in jumping some pretty high hurdles.

Someone has said, "If God tells you to get on the other side of that impossible looking wall, it's your job to get up to the wall and it's God's job to get you over."

During our second trip to Canada, we had this principle vividly illustrated. We were on our way from Toronto, Ontario, Canada to Winnipeg, Manitoba, Canada, where we had been invited and many appearances had already been arranged for us to sing and quote the Bible.

We were driving out Bloor Street leaving Toronto and Ma turned to Dad with a gentle look of concern on her face asking, "Do we really have enough money to get all the way to Winnipeg? It's fifteen hundred miles you know." With both hands firmly grasping the steering wheel and shoulders squared, he set his countenance solidly and with only the slightest trickle of rebuke said, "My dear, we have enough money to go as far as God wants us to go. My calculations tell me we'll get these eight kids and the three cars about half way. From there on, I don't calculate, I just trust God."

I guess my mother reasoned there wasn't any use trying to argue with that statement, so the conversation quickly faded off, and Mother went back to teaching Peter (eight yrs. old) his school lessons as the three car caravan continued toward Winnipeg.

It was very unfortunate, in Peter's estimation, to be in the same car with his mother, for he had a deathly hatred at this age for studying and was constantly using all the tricks he could muster to see that the teacher was in one car and he was in another. Actually, on several occasions he succeeded because our mother, teacher, overseer was so busy with so many other things that Peter could easily get out of sight, which is usually out of mind, by climbing to the bottom of a blanket box or some other hiding place in the other two cars.

If anybody had been around and heard us mention that we expected to travel fifteen hundred miles in the three old chariots we were driving, I'm sure they would have laughed as hard at us as they did at Noah when he built his ark on the desert. However, we as children in these important formative years were being indelibly impressed with the fact that what men have to say is not nearly as important as what God says. What mattered right here and now was that God indicated that He wanted ten people to travel fifteen hundred miles in three old cars and that with only half of the money needed.

When God commissioned Moses to go and free the captive Israelites from the evil tyranny of Pharaoh, Moses faltered under the premise that he was not eloquent enough. "And the Lord said unto him, Who hath made man's mouth? Or who maketh the dumb, or deaf, or the seeing, or the blind? Have not I the Lord? Now therefore go, and I will be with thy mouth, and teach thee what thou shalt say." Unfortunately, Moses did not trust God enough at this time to let God speak through him and help him overcome his inherited weakness of being "slow of speech and of a slow tongue," and consequently the Bible records that the "anger of the Lord was kindled against Moses."

We were not very "eloquent" financially but God gave Father the faith to go on in spite of what men might say or do. So regardless of what people say, if you as one individual will accomplish God's will for you, your life will carry much more thrill and excitement than if you choose the path of least resistance when all the cards are stacked against you. I have proven this and I hope you will.

"I have seen the wicked in great power, and spreading himself like a green bay tree. Yet he passed away, and, lo, he was not: yea, I sought him, but he could not be found. Mark the perfect man, and behold the upright: for the end of that man is peace. But the transgressors shall be destroyed together: the end of the wicked shall be cut off. But the salvation of the righteous is of the LORD: he is their strength in the time of trouble. And the LORD shall help them, and deliver them: he shall deliver them from the wicked, and save them, because they trust in him." (Psalm 37:35-40)

We drove out of Canada and headed across the top of the United States through Michigan and halfway through Minnesota.

When Dad had spent his last dollar and we were almost out of gas, six hundred miles remained between Winnipeg, Manitoba and the Pent family who had been advertised all over town to sing and preach. What a lonely feeling as night came on and the shadows got longer to think of ourselves out in the middle of nowhere with no friends (or even enemies) to make us feel at home, no familiar bed to crawl into, no supper waiting on the table, no nothing! Paul, Elisabeth, Connie, and I then ranged between 14 and 20 yrs. old and all started wondering out loud as to whether we would soon be ending up out on some lonely country road out of gas and out of food. These experiences made us dig into the Bible even more and taught us to trust God without reserve. A verse that fit our case perfectly and gave us additional strength we read from Joshua 1:9, "Have not I commanded thee? Be strong and of a good courage; be not afraid, neither be thou dismayed: for the Lord thy God is with thee withersoever thou goest."

It was twenty minutes after seven on Wednesday night as we drove into a Minnesota town. Though no contacts had ever been made here, Father decided to find a good church and go to prayer meeting. I think that was a good idea. Of course we don't just pray when we are in great need but being very realistic, the only way we were going to get out of this situation was to pray our way out. "I called upon the Lord in distress: the Lord answered me, and set me in a large place." It is better to trust in the Lord than to put confidence in man. It is better to trust in the Lord than to put confidence in princes." Psalm 118:5,8,9

After phoning around town for a few churches, Dad came back to report that praying wasn't thought of very much, for only a few churches seemed to meet.

We finally located a Baptist church that was enthusiastic about praying and we walked in and introduced ourselves to a deacon standing at the door. We were twenty minutes late, but they marched us right up to the front seat and sat us down. In a few minutes we heard our name being called and the minister asked Father to tell where we were from and give a testimony, then sing for them. Evidently the Holy Spirit was doing work in everybody that night because they had never seen us before and did not know what we sang or how we sang it.

We very gladly put all the energy we could muster into our best song and gave a short testimony, without mentioning anything about our current situation.

33

After the meeting was over, everyone greeted us warmly and praised us for the wonderful work we were doing and said they thought it was wonderful that a family could stay together and work together like this. Little did they know as we stood chatting amiably with smiles on our faces that we were broke, penniless and homeless. We were in the process of learning that the average person in this twentieth century is accustomed to having a regular income and thinking that all others have the same. When a traveling missionary or family like ours comes along, most people think, "Well, they must have guaranteed support by several groups, or they just couldn't keep going like that."

Practically everyone had gone home and my discouragement was beginning to get the upper hand. I walked out into the night and sat in the car, waiting for the whole family to get together for one of our "big ten" conferences to see what we would do next. (I'll tell you one thing; I sure didn't have any ideas on what to do or where to go.) After waiting five minutes, I breathed a weak, discouraged prayer asking the Lord if He could help us a little, and then got impatient and walked back into the church. As I entered, I heard a gentle lady's voice over in the corner by the cloakroom but couldn't see her. However, David, Daddy, Connie, Liz, Paul, and Ma were all standing in a circle back there so I sauntered over to see a short little lady in the middle of them all. She was slightly built with a motherly look of kindness on her glowing face. She did have a few wrinkles but they were soft and gentle and actually added a subtle hint of graciousness to her personality.

You just can't imagine how many leaps my heart took as I neared the group and heard her saying, "I so wish you could come over and spend the night at my house. My husband is retired and we have plenty of room for

everybody and we'll have a great time together." It took
about one deep breath to generate the enthusiasm she was
showing, and we all jumped into the cars and headed for
"home." On the way over to the house there were three
carloads of thanksgiving services with the Lord, telling
Him how we appreciated the way He provided for our
every need and had answered so many of our requests.

It didn't take us long as we neared their home
to see that we would be staying in a very fashionable
neighborhood. The only things that didn't quite fit in this
beautiful place were our three old travel beaten cars, but we
couldn't have cared less what fit where. We were too tired,
thankful, and happy to be thinking about styles.

The next morning after a good breakfast we still had
one big problem. How were ten people and three cars going
to get six hundred miles to Winnipeg, Manitoba by Saturday
night on no money? (It was now Thursday morning.) If
that doesn't sound like much of a problem, you just try it
sometime and you'll agree that it presents quite a challenge.

After pondering this problem and having our morning
devotions in an upstairs bedroom, a phone call came
asking us to stay until Friday night. The message said they
would like us to sing at a big teenage rally. The message
didn't stop there though. It went on to say they were hard
up financially and wouldn't be able to give us anything
whatsoever in the way of financial assistance. We had heard
this predicament at other times and I don't think it bothered
my father and some of the older ones, but for some of the
younger ones and me who at that time could only see the
circumstances, it looked like a mighty discouraging deal.

Bible verses like Isaiah 50:10 and 51:14-16 which
Dad and Ma depended upon so much at times like
these formerly passed through our minds without much

35

significance until experiences like this made us sit up and listen, and our young minds realized that we were in this together and there was a lot at stake.

"Who is among you that feareth the Lord, that obeyeth the voice of his servant, that walketh in darkness, and hath no light? Let him trust in the name of the Lord, and stay upon his God." "The captive exile hasteneth that he may be loosed, and that he should not die in the pit, nor that his bread should fail. But I am the Lord thy God, that divided the sea, whose waves roared: The Lord of hosts is his name. And I have put my words in thy mouth, and I have covered thee in the shadow of mine hand..."

Our host and hostess encouraged us to stay over and gladly offered their home to us.

After praying that the Lord's will be done, Dad gave the O.K. and we made preparation to stay for the Friday program.

We were given the first thirty minutes of the rally and filled it with lively performances of singing, using a cappella, as well as instrumental numbers and a dramatic presentation of the story of Daniel in the lions' den by David (then 24 years old).

After hearing this, the special speaker of the evening decided to give us his speaking time too, so we continued another forty minutes.

After we had finished, the master of ceremonies came up and told the audience that he really appreciated a program of this caliber and knew that the young people did too, and if there was anybody that would like to contribute to our work, there would be an offering plate at each door. I can remember how my heart started beating a real fast thump, thump, thump, against my chest and after the dismissal, each of us looked around with large smiles, fully believing that victory was near and so was Winnipeg.

Of course we wouldn't know until the next day when the treasurer brought the offering around. It might be two dollars or two hundred dollars, it was impossible to predict because of the nature of the meeting and since the majority were teenagers.

The next morning, the treasurer appeared at the door with the offering. After he had left, Dad sent Peter and Timothy scurrying through the three-story house to round up his wife and children to tell them the news he had received from the treasurer.

As they started arriving from various sections of the house to the little bedroom at the top of the stairs, you could sense a wide range of moods as each one entered the door.

Ma came in quite quickly and sat on one of the twin beds with a hint of anxiousness portrayed on her smooth, unwrinkled face. Dave isn't the type that portrays his feelings through facial expressions, so it's hard to analyze his mood except to say he looked as solid as the heart of an oak and ready for any news that was coming. Connie was already sitting in an armchair wishing the slowpokes would hurry up so she could hear what Dad had to say. I'm the curious one in the family and nosy at times, so I met the treasurer at the door as soon as he arrived and this was no news to me, but I was present because the reaction to the news would be of interest and besides, this was a general summons for another "big ten" conference. Liz came in smiling with a look of utter trust in everything and everybody. Paul, who had not yet gotten around to combing his hair and who went to the barber every two months whether he needed it or not, strode in, displaying his tousled mop and making a facial expression hard to decipher except for his typically determined chin that was always set solidly and somehow expressed his mood with

37

the thought, "We'll get through this somehow." Then Peter and Timothy appeared in the doorway with a triumphant look on their young faces, not necessarily because each one had come at their beckoning, but more in the fact that their youngest sister Charlotte, with a "please don't rush me" attitude, was ahead of them whom they had prodded up the stairs and now appeared stumbling through the doorway with Peter and Timothy close at her heels.

The room was silent except for breathing and Dad, who had been concentrating his thoughts on another item of business, suddenly realized he was surrounded with people and looked around to see if each one was there.

Without a lot of fanfare of introduction he simply said, "The Lord sent us in money last night that will be more than sufficient to get us to Winnipeg and I think we should bow our heads and thank Him for answering our prayers and seeing us through this trial."

The room immediately broke into chatter as each one voiced a different set of syllables but all in effect were glad at the prospect of being on the way again and that God had once more honored His Infallible Word in that He would supply all our needs "according to His riches in glory by Christ Jesus." (Philippians 4:19) After each one had thanked the Lord for these blessings, we were dismissed for packing the three cars.

Saturday night, there we were, singing to a packed house in Winnipeg and preaching the Good News of Christ's death and resurrection for sinners. All the hardships, doubts and fears of the trip paled into insignificance as more than 200 of that audience made a solemn promise to God that from then on, the Bible would be read regularly in their homes. In addition, and equally thrilling, was the fact that fifteen people who had never before found that Jesus Christ was their only means of Salvation from sin, indicated they would trust Christ as Lord and Savior. And just to think, that was only the first night there. If we were to have gone home right then, it would have been worth all the sweat, tears, and struggle. What a thrilling life! The prophet Jeremiah who lived six hundred years before Christ appeared on the earth, realized how thrilling it was to follow the Lord and do His perfect will when he profoundly stated in Jeremiah 10, "It is not in man that walketh to direct his steps." And Jesus said, "Come unto me all ye that labor and are heavy laden, and I will give you rest; Take my yoke upon you, and learn of me; for I am meek and lowly in heart: and ye shall find rest unto your souls. For my yoke is easy, and my burden is light." (Matthew 11:28-30)

4

Business in the Buggy Truck

Any man who wants to travel extensively and especially with his family in this day and age must have a pretty good income and know where his money will be coming from and how much he can expect regularly. Any man, that is, except my father. Not only did he manage to get himself around, but from his marriage until now he has never ever left us to go anywhere on a trip by himself. We always go with him, sometimes gratefully, sometimes grudgingly, but still, always!

His driving determination to preach and encourage other families to live Godly lives has never died, and to this day he is on the go and most of the time men twenty years younger find it a very fast and rugged pace. He keeps saying, "We've only seventy or eighty years at the most to lay up our treasure in Heaven where we can enjoy it for all Eternity and when I get there I want to really have something." Then he pounds on the nearest thing handy and says, "Everything you'll enjoy in God's Eternal empire for the millions of years to come depends entirely on how you work for God now! "Then using the same method as he used to prove all his other points, he starts off on a ream of Scripture verses to back up his claims. For this subject I've often heard him start in like this: "The Lord says, 'Not even a cup of cold water given in my name shall in any wise lose its reward;' and, 'Every man shall be rewarded according to his labor;' (not according to his laziness) and 'Behold, I come quickly and my reward is with me to give to every man according as his work shall be.'"

To practice what he preached about working and earning rewards that God had promised in the Bible, he would go out after he finished preaching services (when people didn't give enough to support him) and put his preaching into practice.

During the days of the great Depression when many preachers were standing religiously aloof from manual labor, he went out and sold evergreen trees and plant food, telling all preachers, "If the great Apostle Paul was forced to make tents during his ministry because people would not support him, I count it a privilege to be able to follow his example and gain the rewards for earning the expenses as well as doing the preaching"

He not only kept body and soul together by his earnings but started winning many of his customers to Christ, giving them the Gospel in his work clothes rather than in a white collar and black suit, as he would have had to do coming to them as a preacher.

During one ten year period, he sold over one million evergreen spruce trees and that ten years included the Depression period. Not only did evergreens start growing but a whole host of new Christians who came to a saving knowledge of Christ as he made out a bill of sale for the trees.

During the earlier years before we children were in our teens and the family ranged from twelve year old David to Paul, four years old, we traveled from Maine to Florida each year. Winters were spent in Florida and summers in Maine and meetings were conducted on the trips back and forth in various churches along the way up and down the East coast.

We owned a little brown house by a little lake outside of Orlando, Florida and all who were old enough went to public school, while Father earned money to keep us all fed.

One day, we came home from school to find parked in our yard a great big old black chauffeur model Pierce Arrow car complete with twelve cylinders, seating for nine, and a winding window rigged in back of the front seat to separate chauffeur from passengers in the rear. It also had a microphone so that communication between the chauffeur and passengers was possible when desired.

Naturally, we all immediately asked Father what this beastly looking monstrosity was going to be used for. He explained with glee that he had gotten the whole thing for one hundred and fifty dollars and that it was going to the body shop tomorrow to have the back cut down and make it usable for a pick up truck. He said, "This will be just what we need to transport trees and fertilizer to our customers around the city."

At the body shop they took a blowtorch and cut the roof off right in back of the front seat and took all the seats out of the middle section. Two days later as we rounded the bend in the road from school, there it sat, blandly demolishing any trace of fineness there may have been at our abode and immediately gained the undivided attention of any passerby.

Paul, then four years old, upon seeing it for the first time said, "Whose buggy truck is that?" So from then on it was officially called "the buggy truck." It certainly ceased to be a car after being cut down and it was far from a real truck, but it surely fit right into the category of a full-fledged "buggy." So the name became common around the house and it was "buggy truck" this and "buggy truck" that from then on.

The next day home from school as we rounded the bend in the road it was still there, only Father was in it and had the motor roaring. "Hurry up," he said, "and get into your work clothes, we've got some jobs to do." So, since it was such a novelty to ride in her, we excitedly got ready and went to work that day. Of course, whenever we went to work with Father we knew, no matter what form it took, it would be good, hard, down to earth, strenuous work.

A sample of one afternoon's work would be to load up a thousand pounds of raw fertilizer materials, which were dumped into the belly of the buggy truck. David and I would take turns, down in the pit, mixing various materials together in preparation for spreading on lawns and shrubs. This was formerly the middle and the back seats, which were removed for this process of mixing and many hours were spent in a half crouched position, mixing fertilizer. If we ever slacked up during the job, Father would always come out with, "Remember fellows, 'Whatsoever thy hand findeth to do, do it with thy might;'" and on down we would go again, shoveling and heaving the stuff fore and aft, getting it ready for the next job.

Anybody watching from a distance could only see what used to be an old car except that its top had been completely severed to the bottom of the windows. As we endeavored to mix up our batch of materials, soft billowing clouds of fertilizer dust, in wave after breath choking wave

came drifting o'er the earth as David or I crouched in the pit with a handkerchief tied to the nose.

As Father drove over hill and dale we would raise and lower big coal shovels full of fertilizer in almost automatic animation to get it mixed by the time we reached the next customer's yard.

Every five minutes or so the dust and heat coupled with sagging back and tired limbs would force our sweating faces and lime dusted heads out of the pit and into the open fresh air, only then to duck back into the pit again, partly as a duty but mostly in bashful amazement at discovering we were driving through town or by our schoolyard where we were already too well known by this big black belching monster.

Not only would fertilizer be billowing from the center, but there was always a generous amount of black exhaust in the rear and under the motor, and several shrubs or bushes for delivery crazily balanced on the old fashioned running boards.

To put it frankly and unmistakably, all this appreciation and capacity for doing God's work in God's will (mixing fertilizer in a pit is doing God's work in God's will if He tells you to do it) came about firstly by the reading of the Bible from earliest youth each day; secondly, by a definite direction of our activities in the formative years; thirdly, and a very persuasive force in our lives, a stick applied to the right place at the right time; fourthly, and very important: upon satisfactory completion of a job, reward in the form of sincere appreciation or material gain or sometimes both.

"Whatsoever thine hand findeth to do, do it with thy might" was the motto, and Mother and Father were, and in fact still are, that motto in living dynamic example.

After a while as we sold more and more trees, people would ask how we got such healthy stock and beautiful color. Rather nonchalantly, Father replied that it was done by blending nine elements which we found all soils basically needed for good results. Consequently, requests started coming in for our blend of: Nitrogen, Phosphate, Potash, Manganese, Iron, Zinc, Copper, Boron, and Magnesium. Immediately Father secured a suitable container, packaged the nine elements and called it "Number One Plant Food."

As time passed and more and more of the so called Christian people cooled toward the idea of giving help to God's servants in the ministry, many times we found ourselves not only doing all the preaching but also doing most of the supporting by earning the money ourselves, but never did we stop ministering. That always came first and foremost and the Lord always blessed us for it. We have proven time and time again the truth of that promise in the Bible, which states, "Seek ye first the kingdom of God and his righteousness; and all these things will be added unto you."

It seems now that many times God directed my father to go to areas where they just weren't taught to give as God expects, or if they were taught, they surely didn't respond to the teaching. After many a trip was through, we might have been in a different part of the world but still under the financial barrel and looking up to the bottom. (This situation on the financial ladder is officially documented as being two rungs lower than "at the bottom of the barrel," and one rung lower than financially embarrassed.) But no matter what the family financial situation happened to be, Dad never presented us with a gloomy picture. He would remind us that serving God meant living on both sides of the tracks and at the present time we were being taught about the other side. He continued encouragingly, "The great Apostle Paul told us, 'I know both how to abound

46

and to suffer need. I can do all things through Christ which strengtheneth me.'"

Many times he would tell us, "If you need anything, just ask for it and God will supply it, and if you want something that you don't necessarily need, obey the verse that states, 'Delight thyself in the Lord and he shall give thee the desires of thine heart.'" I can tell you from experience that it really works. Of course the key to the situation is how to really delight yourself in the Lord. You might obey the first clause, "delight thyself in the Lord," before you can realize the second, "he will give thee the desires of thine heart".

One time during extensive meetings in schools where donations and offerings were always the lowest, we could see that if we were going to eat during that week something had to be done. So Father registered our plant food with the particular state where we were, and got a license to sell nursery stock. At the end of a two-week period we not only had given the Gospel to hundreds of teenagers, but also had earned over $700. God so helped us in the time that was left over from the meetings that we seemed to hit all the best prospects and were able to keep ahead of our heavy expenses.

Whenever money was needed, you'd see Father drive in to the house or motel where we were staying with big boxes of cartons. It just so happens that the one-gallon cylindrical ice cream containers that were used so commonly used years ago were the perfect thing to put our blend of plant food into. Also, through God's providence, a beautiful four-color label was purchased at a fraction of the cost of our competitors and the label on the box made a very neat package. As soon as Father drove in and we saw those cartons, we knew we were in for some good hard work. He would jump out of the car and give his high shrill whistle which nobody in the world could copy accurately and no matter where you happened to be or what you were doing, that meant in no uncertain terms that you were to drop everything and run to headquarters.

As soon as everybody arrived (usually in about thirty seconds flat) the orders started flying a mile a minute.

Just before everybody separated to carry out the assignments, he would pray and ask God to supply the needs and then we were off.

The boxes were brought in and Connie, Elisabeth, Charlotte, and Ma would glue the color labels on the boxes, making them ready for the filling process.

While they were doing that Father, David, Arnold III, Paul, Peter, and Timothy would take the truck and go buy the raw materials that were needed for the mixture. (Some of the materials we couldn't buy and had to carry quite a quantity with us because it was available from a very distant source.)

As soon as we got back from the blending plant everybody worked at setting up the assembly line for the actual process of packaging while Father went and asked the motel or apartment manager if it would be all right to use part of his drive-way for fifteen or twenty minutes.

After clearance from that angle we were ready to swing into action. By this time everybody had his orders and knew exactly what to do.

Whether you were viewing at a distance or close up, the whole process had a striking similarity to a busy anthill on a spring day the way each one feverishly did his job.

Connie and Charlotte would uncap the containers and hand them to David and Dad who were holding each box in place, as Paul and I would pour the mixture from the bags. Then from there they were handed to Elisabeth and Tim who would cap them and toss them to Peter and Ma who put them in packaging boxes for shipments elsewhere to good customers or for local distribution.

Being in a different city or town every week or month sometimes presented seemingly insurmountable problems. For instance, how can you get all this done without raising suspicions of the many nosy people who wander around these days tending to everybody's business but their own?

I must admit it looked rather strange to see ten people working like all guns outside a motel or in a driveway and other like places. However, it had to be done and the Lord helped us take care of the busybodies.

We hadn't done it very long though when most of us got used to it, and as people would stop and watch in wonderment at what was happening, we would show how proficient we were and start tossing with great agility, full cans of fertilizer to the next one on the assembly line.

Fortunately we had the sense to make sure everything was done according to the local laws about registering, licensing, etc. so that there was a very minimum of trouble along this line.

One time we were out in front of a motel in Michigan all working up a storm with cans and caps flying through the air, people running hither and thither doing their job, and Dad standing near by hollering reams of orders to keep things flowing smoothly; when all of the people to drive up—a state trooper on daily patrol. With a natural instinct for checking on heavy commotion he screeched to a stop and stared at this intensely mixed up scene. Instead of questioning us for twenty or thirty minutes (which did happen more than once), since we weren't breaking any laws, he just sat there and stared with jaw lowered, tongue hanging out and eyes straining at the sockets.

In a few minutes, when he got tired of watching us

and our antics he shook his head in a wondering sort of way and drove on to a more lucrative section of the city.

As soon as the plant food had been packaged and all necessary licenses obtained, we would hit the city with an irresistible sales talk and a week later have enough to go and preach somewhere else.

Of course, a lean week of selling would sometimes stifle progress and Dad's familiar statement again went ringing through the house, "Everybody bring all you've got and put it on the table and we'll see what our resources are."

This meant nothing else than to empty your pockets of all Uncle Sam's treasures including pocket change, wallet money, and any savings hidden in secret corners and invisible locations.

As we would "shell out," Father stood over against the treasury quoting verses of Scripture: "She gave all that she had," "The Lord loveth a cheerful giver," "Every man as he purposeth in his heart, so let him give; not grudgingly!"

After everybody had parted with every cent he had, and it was all counted on the table we would all gather around and pray that the Lord would make it go to meet our needs. (It always did or the Lord supplied more.)

Beside our business of selling trees and plant food, there were always offerings (almost always) and they helped in getting us around. Sometimes the offerings were very good and sometimes very poor. As the free will offerings were counted sometimes the churches would add to our offering from their treasury and sometimes churches would take from our offerings and add to their treasury.

It didn't bother us as much when the congregation we were ministering to was poor or low on finances. What really irked us was when a church would lead the audience to believe that the entire offering was going to us and then just give us a small honorarium. (Father liked to call them dishonorariums.) This happened several times and the churches that did it always were the losers for it, because God had promised to supply our needs and whether the local church did its share or not, it may have hindered us a little but it never stopped us from preaching.

One church, I remember especially, was where we were having some very successful meetings and the pastor was seemingly friendly and cooperative. On the Sunday night service the church was packed and the pastor stepped up to take the offering. During the day he had noticed that Peter (then ten years old) had a hole in the sole of his shoe.

After saying a few words, he stopped and turned to Peter and said, "Let me see your shoe a minute." So Peter pulled off his shoe right on the platform and the preacher held it up, poked his finger through the hole so everybody could see, and said, "Now, I want you to help this fellow get a good pair of shoes. He evidently needs them and I'm wondering who in the audience would be willing to put ten dollars in the offering to buy shoes for Peter." Four people raised their hands. "All right that's fine, now everybody give a good offering to keep these wonderful people going."

After everything was packed and we were about on our way, the preacher handed Father an envelope which he put in his pocket, and we drove off. After getting out of town and down the road a few miles, Father opened the envelope and found a check for the grand sum of ten dollars.

As we looked back on the long drive we had made to come, and the hours of preparation that went into the program, sweat began to appear on our foreheads and feelings of the most unkind nature crept over our beings. When we started to express them verbally, Father reminded us that the Judge of all the earth would do right, not only in punishing the guilty but rewarding those who had done their best, and that the Lord had said, "Vengeance is mine; I will repay saith the Lord."

Whenever these things happened, never once did we mention a word about it, either to the preacher or anyone else. There were times, however, when we almost yielded to the temptation and gave them a piece of our mind.

One time especially was at a beautiful big church where one Sunday night the church was packed with many hundreds of people. In the middle of the meeting the pastor took ten minutes exonerating us and our "wonderful work." Then he told his people to really help this wonderful family because the whole offering was going to them.

At the close of the program, many gave their lives to Christ. As Father walked out of the church when everything was over, one of the deacons handed him fifteen dollars.

When we all got back to our motel that night we discussed what should be done, but everybody was of the generally heated opinion that Dad should phone the pastor of the church and remind him of his offering announcement during the meeting.

So Dad did go to a telephone and dialed the number. Nobody answered. He tried again and still no answer.

Then he came back to us and said, "You know, I don't think that God would have me call this man. Let's let the Lord take care of punishing him and we'll keep going." We were all quite disappointed but have always been glad that he didn't say anything.

The Bible promises in Psalm 1, talking about the man who delights himself in the law of the Lord, "Whatsoever he doeth shall prosper," and even though some of us were disappointed then, we can see that since we were endeavoring to do God's will, He prospered us after that in spite of the failings of men.

During those years, we learned some valuable lessons about trusting God alone and not pinning our hopes of prosperity and success on mere men.

No matter how good they might be or where their successes had taken them, we all learned through the daily reminders of personal experience and Scriptures quoted to us by Father that complete trust in the Lord was the only solid foundation to build our lives on. "Put not your trust in princes, nor in the son of man in whom there is no help." (Psalm 146)

"Lean not on thine own understanding, in all thy ways acknowledge Him, and He shall direct thy paths." (Proverbs 3)

5

Snoring Through the Keyhole

"For, lo, he that formeth the mountains, and createth the wind, and declareth unto man what is his thought, that maketh the morning darkness, and treadeth upon the high places of the earth, the LORD, the God of hosts, is his name." (Amos 4:13)

The Canadian Rockies hold some of the most majestic scenery that you will see anywhere in the world.

When you first drive into Banff, Alberta, the mountains seem so high, rugged and magnificent, you can't help but be greatly stirred by such an awe-inspiring experience.

Thousands of feet into the air, these jagged hewn clefts stand solid and erect against the soft billowing clouds, while at your feet rushes a pure mountain stream sending cool clear water cascading over small cliffs and rushing to the beautiful expanse of green lakes far below.

As you stand there and look at this handiwork that only God could fashion, you cannot help but ponder His greatness, the wonderful fact of His being, and begin to realize His true and unequalled glory.

"Mine hand also hath laid the foundation of the earth, and my right hand hat spanned the heavens: when I call unto them, they stand up together." (Isaiah 48:13)

Almost everybody dreams of having a vacation in a

spot like this, where you seem to almost be in another world, and I consider this no wonder now that I look back on it. It was our good providence to be able to spend a whole month of solid vacation in these Canadian Rockies.

This was the first vacation we had had for over two and a half years and it did us all a world of good.

It would not have been practical to travel way up there except that we were invited by a youth organization to make a thirty day tour through the province of Alberta, Canada, which we gladly did. The tour was very successful. One of the directors told us the crowds that gathered in the various cities and towns were, in most cases, twice as large as anything they had ever seen. We were most thankful for the great response to the invitations. Many scores gave their hearts to Christ and received the great gift of Eternal Life.

However, though it was very rewarding, it was also very hard. We had a program every night in a different town and of course slept in a different home each night, with everybody trying to out-do or out-shine the other town in hospitality: which resulted in a big breakfast, a bigger dinner, and a huge evening meal. Then to top it all off, the Canadians have a custom of having what they term, "a little lunch before they go to bed." This little lunch consists of practically everything I've ever seen or heard of in the realm of food being spread on the table and you fill up...at least they filled up. As soon as we could get away from the meeting we would find where our bed was located, greet our host and hostess very cheerfully, and before they fully realized we were even there, we would be under the covers and on our way to sleep. They thought we were washing up or something and when we never showed up after going into our room, they would knock on the door and say, "Come on boys, it's time for a little lunch." We either politely told them a little sleep was more necessary or just snored real loud through the key hole and they would get the point and eat their "little lunch" alone.

During this thirty-day tour we had over forty programs. Most of the traveling was on dusty gravel roads, except of course when it rained and then it was exclusively over muddy roads. We had eleven flat tires. Halfway through the tour two axles broke on the same car and a plane had to fly us replacements from 2,000 miles away. This was because the Canadian-built Pontiac car was not exactly like our American Pontiac but was half Pontiac and half Chevrolet, so their Canadian axle didn't fit our American car.

However, after $176.00 and some precious time consumed, we resumed speed and finished in good shape.

Even though the whole thing was rather difficult and arduous labor, we enjoyed every minute of it and will never forget the wonderful way the Canadians treated us. We got to know many of them quite well and really appreciated their conservative type of life and their conservative beliefs.

We had been looking forward to and planning our vacation in the Canadian Rockies for quite a while now and the time had finally come.

We rented two bungalows perched 300 feet above the town of Banff, Alberta, Canada and had a vacation for one solid month. It was really a refreshing experience to be tucked away where nobody could find us. It only cost us seven dollars per night and was very inexpensive in comparison to other places we had been, with much more inferior surroundings.

Our meals averaged thirty-five dollars a week for all ten people, and you know that's almost unbelievable in this day and age. We were able to do it by eating meat once a week and then buying inexpensive but nourishing food the rest of the time. Fresh vegetables with real butter, home made, whole wheat bread, milk, honey, and fruit was our main diet; and only thirty-five dollars a week. That figures out to be only ten and a half cents per meal per person and we were completely satisfied and stayed perfectly healthy the whole time.

Among other things, we hiked up steep mountainsides, rode tandem (two seat) bicycles, and just rested.

This is the type of country where you can take a walk through the woods and meet elk, deer, moose, wolves, bears, and many other kinds of wildlife.

Believe me, it really adds a lot of spice to your daily exercise when you're calmly walking along a mountain trail and just as you come around the corner one way, two black bears come around the corner the other way.

They looked so innocent and lovable it didn't seem like they could hurt a flea. On second thought, we remembered how the ranger told us about the man that tried to engage one, and the bear lifted one mighty paw and knocked his head from his body. Stories like this are actually true and a little voice inside told us we better run, and do it fast.

So we did run, and did it fast while the bears stood there with a funny look in their eyes as if to say, "What ever got into them?"

After we had put a healthy distance between us and them, everything went back to normal as we continued our little hike over the beautiful forested trail. That is until we rounded another bend and saw a whole herd of white tailed deer quietly munching on some grass. Unlike the bears, who will stand all day and look you over, these swift creatures, at the cracking of one branch, will dart into the woods never to be seen again. And so it happened, and we never saw them again.

On our thirty-day tour, we met a leading Canadian lecturer whose business was traveling around the world, filming its scenic, historic, and mysterious high spots.

It caught his eye one day when he saw us advertised as the "World's Most Unusual Family." He invited us to come to what is described as the most beautiful spot in the world. He explained that he was a Christian and he desired to get a Christian testimony across to his large audiences and thought that since the title of his next film was "Around the World in 24 Days" it would fit perfectly to have the "World's Most Unusual Family" as part of the story.

So he arranged to meet us at a certain place on a certain day when we would drive to the filming location known as "the most beautiful spot in the world."

We entered the Canadian Rockies on a beautiful sunny day and drove higher and higher into the mountains. Finally, reaching an elevation of 7,000 feet we came upon the most beautiful scenery you have ever laid eyes on. It just about defied description. When I say "just about" I mean that I can't describe it in all its glory.

We climbed a mountain trail by foot into the primeval forests over 2,000 more feet upward. On the way up we crossed small mountain streams, which had their source at the top of the snow-capped mountain. Since the sun was shining and the weather very warm, it didn't take too long to work up some perspiration, and what could be more refreshing than to cool your face in a cold mountain stream?

After our 2,000 foot climb, we turned around and saw far below us, beautiful Lake Moraine with its almost fluorescent green hue, and stately evergreens growing right to the water's edge.

In the center of the picture was a huge white glacier with snow being reflected in the lake, over 600 feet deep. This huge glacier came from between two high snow capped mountains and extended right down to the lake. These glaciers were simply huge mountains of snow and ice, slowly but persistently pushing their way over the earth and covering everything in their path. In this case, the

glacier extended inch by inch over the surface of the lake
until the weight of the ice reached many tons, and then
cracked off the main glacier and fell into the lake.

To either side of the glacier and thousands of feet into
the air stood eight other world famous mountain peaks,
thickly covered with huge ancient spruce and fir trees, all
towering toward heaven in silent splendor and beauty.

At ten thousand feet, a blanket of snow had fallen and
every capped peak sparkled in the sun. And then below
all of this, the whole scene was again beheld through,
as it were, green tinted glasses, as the smooth, glass-like
surface of the lake reflected the whole panorama in all of its
breathtaking wonder.

After seeing such things as these, our minds went back
to that famous passage in the Bible, "In the beginning
God created the Heavens and the earth," (Genesis 1:1)
and thought how small and insignificant people make
themselves, when they try to minimize the Almighty
power of God and project an analysis of Him that reveals
absolutely nothing: nothing that is, except their puny,
godless imaginations.

By now the world-traveling photographer had all of his
equipment set up and asked that we sing the song, "How
Great Thou Art." The film started rolling and we sang
the song he requested with much enthusiasm under the
inspiration of these moments.

After finishing the filming, we all descended from the
mountain and parted company with the photographer. His
parting comments were, "I would like to feature your family
in my next around the world film and title it, "Around The
World With The World's Most Unusual Family."

We had now spent a month of rest and vacation in
the Canadian Rockies. In two more days we would be

taking off for another one or two or maybe three years of traveling before a real formal vacation was declared again. This sounds worse that it actually is. My father follows very religiously the principle of one day of rest every seven days. When you get in the habit of doing this, your body is able to build up and you can go on indefinitely, and when you enjoy our work as much as we do, there is nothing to it.

Incidentally, this trip we were about to conclude through Canada had an interesting sidelight. We entered Canadian Customs from the New Hampshire border with nine dollars, and after traveling thousands of miles with ten people, three cars, and staying in motels practically every night, Father counted his assets as we crossed the border into Montana and he still had nine dollars.

6

Depth Perception and Diplomacy

On the morning of our departure after being "patriotic" and eating a breakfast consisting of leftovers from a month's stay, we finished packing (it's quite a job to pack after you've been in one house a whole month).

Little did we know what this day held in store for us in the way of time consuming and discouraging circumstances.

After finally getting packed, we weren't on the road thirty minutes before we had a flat tire.

Now for any regular person in the world, changing a tire isn't too hard a job, but with us it's different.

In the first place, to find the tire and get at it was a major operation. Dave put his key in the trunk, turned it, and all of a sudden the trunk lid seemed to jump at him like something possessed. (Of course, that wouldn't be too hard to understand if you had been around at packing time and watched three sweating faces all working together to get it closed.)

After scraping the loose, last minute articles from the top of the load and lifting out suitcases, night bags, shoes, advertising material, records, and instruments, David finally got to the tire which was in the farthest recess of the trunk, tightly screwed to the frame.

At this juncture, things were all taking entirely too long, so Dad stepped into the picture and started the orders flying. "David, you take off the hub cap, Paul, loosen the nuts, Connie, you get a rock under the front wheel and brace the car, Arnold, get the jack, Elisabeth, put on the brakes, and Ma, take Peter, Tim, and Charlotte for a walk, and get them out from under our feet."

In no time flat the job was done and we were all but on our way again. Everybody pitched in to help pack up, and in a shorter time than it takes to turn around twice, the trunk was full and jam packed with not one extra inch to spare anywhere. There was just one slight problem; half of the luggage was still on the ground. Then the master of packing ceremonies came into the picture. "Now listen everybody," said Paul, his voice ringing with confidence, "just take everything out and we'll put this stuff back as we had it before." Everybody cooperated, including Dad, and Paul jumped into the back trunk as each one handed him some suitcases, night bags, shoes, advertising material, records, instruments…in the right order. Some people wonder how we get our education on the road. Well, this is one phase of it right here. Paul was learning depth perception, mathematics, and diplomacy.

Finally everything was ready, and we were breezing down the highway again. Our destination goal was a small town on the U.S.-Canadian border and we calculated that it could be easily reached by 7 that evening.

At noon, we passed through Calgary, Alberta, and stopped to take in a good and typically Canadian meal at the invitation of the world traveling photographer's home. When I mention "typical Canadian" I refer to their abundant variety of food and preparations.

When you think of a typical American meal there is usually one meat, one salad, two vegetables, one drink, and one dessert, but not so with these Canadians. In most of our experiences they have had about three or four salads, two meats, four vegetables, various drinks, and a couple of desserts. Not to mention before dinner olives, after dinner mints, in-between meal snacks, and late "lunches."

After eating, we had a time of devotions together, all giving a favorite verse or passage of Scripture around the table. Father diligently pursued this habit of devotions after breakfast, after dinner, and after supper, no matter where we went. He contends that anyone alive should feed his soul more than he does his body because the soul lives forever and the body decays and dies. And so he set aside these and other definite times not only for our benefit but for those we were with and influenced. Because of being diligent in this habit and showing other families how we carry on devotions, a majority of the families that have invited any or all of us to a meal, write or let us know later that they are now carrying on regular family devotions. "…It is written, Man shall not live by bread alone, but by every word that proceedeth out of the mouth of God." (Matt. 4:4)

An hour and a half later, we were on the road again

heading for the United States border. Everything went smoothly all afternoon and we were enjoying the pleasant weather and the beauty of Canada's rolling plains.

At five o'clock we rolled into a peaceful town seventy miles from the border. This Monday happened to be a Canadian holiday and everybody and everything was nowhere to be found.

For our evening meal, the only thing we could find open was a little grocery store on a narrow back street operated by a Chinaman. After stocking up for a picnic supper, we headed out of town with our eyes open for a good place to stop and eat.

As we turned the corner from a stoplight, there came from underneath the car a strange ticking and grinding sound. It so happened that Elisabeth was in the driver's seat, and Connie, Paul, and I were stacked elsewhere amidst the luggage. We all looked at each other in dismay and bewilderment, recalling that this same sound had made itself heard one month previous on our thirty day tour of Alberta and had turned out to be two broken axles with a repair cost of $176. We were in no mood to go through this experience again and advised Elisabeth to drive slowly and easily to see if something more might develop. The Buick, acting as the lead car during this trip, knew nothing of our predicament and took off from the light and down the street.

Well, sure enough, our ticking and grinding sound developed nicely, until the whole car rattled and shook, so I said, "Liz, you had better pull over or this whole thing is going to fall apart."

None of us knows a lick about mechanics but we all jumped out anyway to see what we could find, and give our appraisal of the situation.

As Connie stuck her inexperienced nose into the front grill work to see if she could smell anything, I looked with eyes of confusion underneath around the differential and muffler section, while Paul poked around the back bumper, pulling on this and pushing on that for loose parts or anything out of the ordinary.

In no time flat we all arose from our inspection with the same ignorant look we had gone down with and decided to wait until the lead car discovered we were missing and came back. Meanwhile, we prayed, asking the Lord to guide us and enable us to get it fixed without a lot of delay and expense.

Finally the lead car noticed we were not with them and came back to find us. Dad immediately got out and came over to see what the trouble was. After sticking his nose in the front grill work to see if he could smell anything, he came back and looked underneath around the differential and muffler section, then poked around the back bumper, pulling on this and pushing on that for loose parts or anything out of the ordinary. In no time flat he arose displaying the popular expression of the moment, coupled with the strain of responsibility. Taking the wheel he drove it around the corner off the highway, listening for the ticking and grinding sound that now came more enthusiastically than ever.

Quite a bit of time had now elapsed and Peter, Timothy, and Charlotte, like baby birds in a nest, were begging for something to fill their vacant stomachs, so Ma dug out the sandwich makings and set up shop on the car seat.

Meanwhile, I was elected to go to the nearest house and phone the garage for a tow truck.

After surveying all the houses of the neighborhood, I picked the most beautiful one I could find. It was a lavishly landscaped and very stately looking place with a beautiful Cadillac standing out front.

A lady of about 60 answered the door and addressed me with a reserved, "who do you think you are" type of hello. I was already feeling very inferior and that greeting really knocked the starch out of me. She must have been staring at me, but I couldn't really tell because the screen door was the "I can see you, but you can't see me" type, so I stated my business with a frightened, far away look as my eyes danced around the big gray screen, trying to find something or somebody to focus upon. After several nervous utterances and trying to frame a smile on my trembling 16-year-old lips, she invited me in.

Mr. "Richman," who had been awakened by the doorbell from his afternoon nap in the living room, was grunting and groaning as he endeavored to raise his spare tire and other accessories to a vertical position. He had evidently been badly defeated in his "battle of the bulge" because as I entered the room he was trying to raise it all over the western slope of the couch. As I explained my plight to him, he picked up the phone and called John Somebody and told him to come over with a tow truck. I tried to explain that the truck had to be an A.A.A. truck because we belonged to that association and received free tows as a service. He seemed to pretend not to hear as he phoned Bob Somebody else and told him to meet him at the garage immediately for a repair job. Well, I wasn't about to be caught with a ten dollar towing bill and some cheating repair job, so I scraped as much courage as I could from the screen door and looking him straight in the eye said, "Are you, or are you not an agent of the A.A.A.?" He looked me straight back and said, "Yes I am, and I own the Pontiac and General Motors dealership here."

After that, to my surprise, he turned out to be very solicitous of our welfare and came outside to see what the matter was.

But by this time, the sandwich making department and its consumers had relocated their base of operation on the front hood and roof of the car and as I approached with this high class gentleman, it looked like the county fair had come to town as everybody paced the sidewalks and grass strip with a glass of milk in one hand and sandwiches in the other, but he seemed to pay no attention to our antics and proceeded to invite us all into his home.

Our car was towed to the Pontiac garage and we found out that we had a repair on our hands that would cost thirteen dollars. That was cheap enough considering what we were expecting, but considering the cash Father had in his pocket, that was something else. So Father walked up to the owner with one little twenty dollar bill in his pocket and said, "I'll be glad to pay you now if you prefer but this was a little unexpected and if it's all the same to you, we could mail it next week from the States." "Why sure that would be perfectly all-right," said the man genially, "I've enjoyed meeting you're whole family. I think you're a very rich man." "Well, thank you," said Father, "we read the Bible each day in our home and it amazes me what the Lord can do in a young person as well as an adult. When these children were very young, Mrs. Pent and I would give them verses like the one over in John 1:12, 'But as many as received Jesus, to them gave he power to become the sons of God, even to them that believe on his name.' Then that one in Romans 10, 'That if thou shalt confess with thy mouth the Lord Jesus, and shalt believe in thine heart that God hath raised him from the dead, thou shalt be saved. For with the heart man believeth unto righteousness; and with the mouth confession is made unto salvation.'"

When the children realized that Jesus Christ offered the gift of Eternal Life, they readily trusted Him to be their Savior and have traveled with us for many thousands of miles singing the Gospel and encouraging other young people to trust Christ as their personal Savior." Then reaching in his pocket, he pulled out the little leaflet we have used for many years with a picture of the family on the front entitled, "Salvation verses from John." "Here, take this and read it. You'll find that Christ does just what He promises and He'll give you Eternal Life if you will believe in Him as

your Savior."

From the time we had been stopped until Dad finished talking with the man three hours had elapsed and we were ready to head for our original destination of Shelby, Montana.

While the repair was being made, Dad had called a motel where we had stayed before in Shelby and reserved two rooms with four double beds. The man on the other end assured us that everything would be ready and waiting.

We arrived in Shelby at one A.M. and were all asleep

except the drivers. The man now on duty informed us that the man who made the reservation for us had seen a little too much of john barley corn. He said there was only one room left containing two double beds.

We had no choice but to take it, and ten sleepy heads piled into a hot, humid, stuffy smelling room.

The manager brought us some extra blankets and everybody picked out a space and guarded it jealously. Believe me, this was no picnic! With ten people in a room thirty by thirty and every inch of bed and floor space covered, once you got in your little nook you stayed there or else, because moving would bring loud squeals from each foot fall you made. By the time I "came to" out in the car and had gotten my suitcase in, the only space left was one corner of the room on the floor, for which I took two blankets from the stockpile. But, alas, it was two feet too short for my frame and I didn't fancy being curled up all night, so I took up my bed and walked to the car, carefully selecting every step between nine other people all stretched out at various angles around the room.

After taking much care in making up a bed in the Buick, I lay down and started to take a good long stretch to rest my sagging muscles, but to my dismay this too was one foot shy of my height. But at this point I was so sleepy and tired of fighting for comfort I just wound down the window and stuck my feet out. Actually, I felt pretty comfortable when I considered the other nine members of the family in that little, hot, sultry room all breathing stale air at each other.

Morning finally came after much tossing and turning and each pursued his daily habit of private Bible reading for one hour before breakfast.

As we were about to leave the motel for our next

destination, the cleaning maid told me a little story that was of particular interest to us all. "You know something," she said, "This morning the boss was furious when he came in and found that the man on duty last night left three spacious rooms unrented." Enough said!

7

Butter and Guns

In my nineteenth year, we took a tour of Michigan, covering forty cities and towns, speaking and singing to audiences ranging from twenty to two thousand. Near the end of the tour, Dad bought a new panel truck that had to be broken in with five hundred miles of slow driving. Paul (17 years old) and I left Central Michigan ahead of the rest of the family and slowly traveled to Eastern Michigan where the family was expected over the weekend for a full round of programs.

Little did we realize on this hot day in July that an event just around the corner would warm our blood far more than any day in July.

Dad had purchased this new one ton panel truck for our musical recordings, literature, clothing and everything else that a family of ten needs.

As we got the feel of the truck loaded for the first time, we noticed that our load was shifting on stops and turns. We decided that as soon as we got into town to go to a lumberyard and have the truck fitted with a partition, which would separate the passengers from the load.

Since there was only one bucket seat on the driver's side, any other passenger had to do the best he could by arranging parts of luggage and load to form his own seat.

I soon found this partition was very necessary, because at the first red light Paul, just getting accustomed to the truck, applied the new power brakes and the boxes, instruments, records, and heterogeneous material cased forward with the make-shift seat, the floor mat, and the yours truly, leaving us all neatly placed in that vicinity rightly named "dashboard".

As soon as we came into the city limits, Paul spotted a lumberyard where we could get the board. The lumberman gladly fit the piece of board partition for us and we drove off to get some dinner.

Abhorring washed out vegetables and greasy meat from some restaurant grill, I suggested to Paul that we go across the street and buy some nourishing food at the super market there.

Leaving the store with a bag full of nourishment Paul said, "Let's just eat over under that shade tree in the corner of the parking lot. So I pulled the truck under the large shade tree and we sat there peacefully enjoying ourselves.

Suddenly I heard footsteps coming from behind the truck in the grass. Then Paul's door swung open and a gruff voice said, "Come out with your hands up high." After Paul's hands went up, a rifle was placed in his back while another partner searched. I was just about to turn white with fear and panic when my door came open and another man said, "Get out and put your hands against the truck!" Seeing the rifle pointed at me and the police badges and three police cars, I decided it would not be in good taste to either panic or run just then.

They looked us over and checked around a bit, then asked me if there were any guns in the truck. I replied that I knew of none except some civil war muskets in the back that were toys of my younger brothers, to which he replied, "Let's see them."

After checking them over and finding them nothing but toys, we came back to the front of the truck and he got a look into the cab where our dinner was spread. When I say spread, I do mean spread, and though making no comment, he stared until his eyeballs were standing out on his cheeks. His reason for staring was not too amazing when you consider what he saw.

On the dashboard was a rye krisp covered with a thick slab of cream cheese and in the cream cheese four olives neatly imbedded in a straight row, just waiting to be eaten. Then he saw a neighboring rye krisp smothering under waves of peanut butter and piled high with raisins and the raisin and peanut butter containers close at hand. Then he saw a can of pineapple juice, then grapefruit juice, then his eyes lighted on some milk and chocolate cookies.

Meanwhile, on the other side of the truck, Paul was still explaining his way out of the realistic looking sawed off shotgun that Peter had bought to play with. The officer looked at it a long time and after a thorough examination found that it was made of sturdy plastic which shot real live plastic bullets.

The policeman then asked Paul if there were any other guns in the truck. To which he replied, "No sir, that's all."

The officer then walked to the back of the panel truck, opened up the doors and out fell some more very realistic looking Civil war muskets which I had showed to the man on the other side of the truck a few minutes before who was questioning me. Paul deemed it best just then to be silent and so did the officer. He looked hard, fiddled, cocked and shot them, and found them perfectly harmless.

The men were finally running out of things to search and ask and started to realize that they'd better start barking jailbirds up in another part of town. It seemed that the party was just about over, and the men all turned and started to walk away.

You can imagine the unusual feeling that must have come over those four husky officers as they walked away with a high powered rifle in one hand and a pistol in the other being watched by two somewhat religious looking fellows and innocent as mother goose. Somebody sure had given them a sorry lead.

Then of all the unfortunate occurrences, one of them remembered that they had not checked our driver's licenses yet. Any other question on any other subject would have been better than this one right now, because when it comes to licenses in our family even we get confused, not to mention the policemen. It so happened that we were driving a truck bearing a Michigan license. This would have been fine if that was all there was to it. However, when we failed to locate the registration proving that we owned the truck and I showed my driver's license from Florida on top of that, then Paul came up with a license from Texas, it was right then and there that they did look at us with thoughts unpleasantly revealed in their eyes.

After these very revealing facts they laid into another juicy round of questions, with them asking a heap too many questions, and us giving a heap too few answers. It was right here that I felt a great need to have a prayer answered and, brother, I prayed to the Lord and asked Him to help us to say the right words.

Some typical questions were, "Who are you anyway?" "What is your business?" "Where are your parents?" "Where did you get this brand new truck?" "Where are you from?" And, "Where are you going?"

To these typical questions we gave very untypical answers and spent most of the time either double talking or filibustering.

Somehow we managed to wiggle past the last two questions without answering them. This was fortunate, because to the question, "Where are you from?", we would have had to reply, "Well sir, we really aren't from anywhere," and then try to explain why we were from nowhere and that we did nothing but travel around the country.

To the question, "Where are you going?", we would have replied, "We are going to Heaven," and then proceed to tell why we were going to Heaven. Some might contend that here was our chance to give a testimony and point them to Heaven. However, when a policeman is staring down his nose at you, and you know that behind that nose he is thinking you are a robber, fraud, and a fast traveler, one deems it wiser to tell the route to Heaven when a more opportune occasion presents itself. It is here that the sage advice of Solomon, "There's a time for every purpose under the sun" be heeded with good results.

To make a long story short, they accepted our few and involved answers and I'm sure the Lord helped convince them that we were all-right because we sure didn't say much to help the situation. Just before they drove off one of the leaders said, "Please fellows, just stay out of trouble."

If you're wondering how all this got started in the first place, the answer is found back at the lumberyard where our helpful "partition fitter" saw this plastic gun behind the seat, and thinking it was a real sawed off shotgun immediately phoned the police because some teen-agers had recently been caught using them and a few more were known to be in the area.

It so happened that our program promoter and arranger in this city was a reporter for the daily news, and Monday was his day for arranging the front page of the newspaper. He got wind of our experience and wrote a good size article, which went in the top right section of the front page and was read all over Northern Michigan.

8

Quoting the Whole New Testament

The phase of our life that sparks much interest and curiosity is how we can stand before thousands of people and quote whole books of the Bible. And yet when you analyze how this is accomplished there is really nothing spectacular in regard to methods of memorizing or systems of retaining this large amount of Scripture.

Of course, some people's minds naturally retain information easier than others and this is so in our family. David and Paul, so far, seem to retain Scripture with greater ease than the rest of us. These two, however, by no means have a corner on Scripture committed to memory. Every other member of the family can quote from a few to several books, depending on age but these two know more books that the rest of us.

David, from the age of 20, has been able to quote the whole New Testament from memory. Naturally with such a large volume, he can't do it word perfect from cover to cover without a little prompting, but if someone were there following through each chapter he could go from cover to cover with very little help.

It's hard for people to believe that he could do this unless he had a photographic memory. However, he does not have a photographic memory and has proven many times that he has the complete New Testament under control.

One time, a teen-ager who had heard he could do this came to him with the express purpose of proving him true or false. So David said, "Just start any verse in the New Testament and I'll finish it for you." The young fellow dug into what he considered the hardest section and started a verse. David with no trouble whatsoever finished the verse and a few more along with it for good measure. Undaunted the fellow started looking again, and again David followed through. After ten minutes of this he began to get a little exhausted and looked into David's eyes with disbelief. David just stood there calmly with his hands behind his back and a small upward curve on his lips.

Then another idea struck the young challenger and he started leafing through the Old Testament with the confidence that he could surely stump him. After samples from Genesis, Isaiah, and Lamentations couldn't bring David down, he just

looked up speechless and walked away. David also—with his wits a little sharper than before went his way.

Then a little later the fellow button-holed Paul and said, "You know, David must be the smartest one in your family. I started verses from all over this Bible and couldn't trip him up once. He quotes these verses better than I can read them. I just can't believe it. How does he ever do it?"

Then Paul folding his arms with an air of confidence and shifting from one foot to the other said in his typically dry wit fashion, "Well that's interesting, maybe you can trip me up. Start any verse you like and we'll see what happens." So again he started in with verse after verse. As Paul finished each one word perfect and the fellow slowed his pace a bit, Paul said, "Now turn over to Matthew one and we'll learn something else." After the fellow had read the verse Paul charged in by memory: "Abraham begat Isaac; and Isaac begat Jacob; and Jacob begat Judas and his brethren: And Judas begat Phares and Zara of Thamar; and Pares begat Esrom; and Esrom begat Aram; And Aram begat Aminadab; and Aminadab begat Naason: and Naason begat Salmon etc."

"You see," said Paul informatively, "the only reason we can do this is because we spend time with it. Thirty minutes of Bible reading after every meal from the time you're born until you're twenty-one is a lot of time. We would all have to be mighty dumb not to know a little something from this book."

One time during one of our tours through Canada we came into a town that was having a large evangelistic crusade. When the evangelist heard that David could quote the New Testament, he invited him to take part in the program and thought the idea of finishing any verse in the New Testament was a splendid one.

So, before an audience of 3,000 people, David finished the verses with rapid-fire precision as people stood from down on the sawdust floor and shouted their verses from all sections of the huge canvas tent.

Everything was going smoothly and there was an air of surprise and admiration as the young man from Florida finished verse after verse. Then one of the preachers on the platform decided to enter in and stood confidently to read from one of the New Testament genealogies where five syllable patriarchs were begetting ten syllable patriarchs. His confidence faded dismally as each name painfully passed his lips sounding more like a sausage coming through the sausage grinder. It was getting so painful, David decided to help him out and finished the whole section from memory. On another occasion, David found himself standing before 2,000 teen-agers who had been given a week's notice to prepare for the encounter. We were trying to encourage them to start memorizing Scripture regularly, so the stipulation was that they quote the first section and David would finish.

These young people were really anxious to get the hardest sections available and were successful, especially in finding parts that were very similar in thought but had a little different wording, such as passages from the four Gospels. David's success was equally good and his confidence and deportment under such great pressure was quite a sight to behold.

When I tell people that we have heard the Bible read for thirty minutes after each meal from the time we were born, they look somewhat surprised and yet I know most people don't realize how much time it really is and the value of making this impression on young minds. Many people have told me that they don't read the Bible to their children because they know the child will not understand it. In fact, many comment that they can't understand it themselves.

My father has told many audiences that educators say a child learns more the first three years of his life than he does in all the rest of his life put together.

"When you mothers talk to your baby in the crib and say, 'Don't cry, Daddy will be home in just a few minutes,' do you think that infant understands Daddy will be home in a few minutes? Of course not! But in six or eight months he'll not only begin to understand it but he'll begin to say it. However, when he is an infant and all you do is smile, coo, and gurgle and fail to communicate the language to him, 6 or 8 months later when the progress should show, there won't be much.

When your child is an infant and you fail to communicate the spiritual language to him by not reading the Bible and not praying in his presence, his understanding and perception of spiritual values will be nothing. He can only begin to understand the Bible when you begin reading it to him and the only reason you can't

TEN P'S IN A POD

understand much of what you read is because you haven't
heard enough yourself."

As soon as each one of us children could talk, we could
talk Scripture. The more we learned to talk the more Scripture
we could give. The Bible says, "Is not my word like as a fire?
saith the Lord; and like a hammer that breaketh the rock in
pieces?" (Jeremiah 23:29) This Bible is a powerful book and
changes for the good all those who are exposed to it.

When Paul was six years old and not yet in school, Mother
would spend time with him during the day when the rest of us
were at school and tell him Bible stories using a flannel graph,
complete with colored pictures. Paul was especially attracted to
the story of Jonah and asked to hear it often.

He was beginning to master the art of reading and
(as with the rest of us as we came to that stage) Father got
him up 30 minutes before breakfast and made him read
the Bible. Since Paul was familiar with the story of Jonah
from the flannel graph and knew the general theme, each
morning at six o'clock when he was awakened, he would
prop himself up on his left elbow, lift two reluctant eyelids
and read the story of Jonah and the fish. The book of
Jonah has four chapters and an average reader can read it
through in seven minutes, but Paul being a beginner found
to his delight that it took him about thirty minutes to get
through it. Every morning as faithful as the sunrise, Jonah
and the fish were swallowed by Paul. However, a great deal
of this faithfulness was Dad's unfailing discipline.

One uneventful morning as we were all sitting in the living
room for family devotions, Paul came in and leaning against
an old living room chair said in a very unassuming manner,
"Well, I learned the book of Jonah." Of course everybody oo'd
and ah'd for a while, then Dad asked him how he did it.

Incidentally, we used to call Paul "Chin Down"

because from 6 to 16 he was very quiet mannered and went around with his chin down, rarely speaking to anyone unless he was spoken to and even then in close cropped statements, deleting all adjectives.

It was unusual enough for him to volunteer the information that he had accomplished this feat, but to have to explain how and when he did it was almost too much. So leaning more heavily against the chair, tilting his head slightly and letting a shy smile escape from his lips he simply said, "In my private devotions before breakfast I have been reading it every morning and well—I just found out I could say it."

Father, immediately turning his Bible over to the book of Jonah said, "We'd like to hear you say it. We'll start morning devotions now and Paul will quote the book of Jonah."

From this moment on in Paul's life, his shyness began to wane and just a few weeks later, he was on television and radio quoting the whole book of Jonah and telling people how he did it.

You probably know the story of Jonah—how he was told by God to go and preach to the wicked Ninevites and Jonah decided he didn't want to go and booked passage on a ship to go to Tarsus instead. Right in the middle of the

voyage, God sent a terrible storm and the shipmates threw Jonah overboard because they learned he had disobeyed God and the sea would be calm again if they got rid of him. Meanwhile, God had prepared a great fish to swallow Jonah and he was in the belly of the fish three days and three nights. The God caused the fish to vomit Jonah up on dry ground and from there he obeyed God, went to Nineveh, and preached that they should repent of their sins.

Incidentally, a result of Paul giving the story of Jonah so frequently in public is that each one in the family can now recite the book from beginning to end.

One time during a tour of New York, there was a rally held in a museum auditorium and Paul was advertised to be there and quote the book. A local promoter of the program came up with this eye-catching slogan and a large article was featured in the paper with this caption, "The boy that swallowed Jonah will be at the museum Saturday night."

Paul's mastery of Jonah, David's of the New Testament, and the rest of us being able to quote many books of the Bible is simply a result of Father's and Mother's determination to keep family devotions going no matter what else came up to interfere. When any of us would complain because we had to spend so much time, he would quote us so many verses proving that it had to be done that one by one we were convinced that he was right.

Just to give you an idea of how much time we really spend in the Bible, here is a breakdown of our schedule and the amount of hours spent from birth to twenty-one years old.

One-half hour of private Bible reading
    from 6-11 yrs..913 hrs.
One hour of private Bible reading
    from 11-21 yrs...3,650 hrs.

Thirty minutes of family devotions after
    each meal from 1-21 yrs old...................11,497 hrs.
Miscellaneous Bible study, prayer time
    and church attendance............................6,000 hrs.
Total time...22,060 hrs.

Father was so determined that we hear the Bible from
infancy, it wasn't a bit unusual, if we happened to be
sleeping, to be awakened out of a sound sleep to hear all
of the family devotions—much to the consternation of
Mother's motherly instincts, believing a baby should get
all its sleep. But we babies didn't have a fighting chance
because Father soon convinced Mother that it was for our
eternal good and the percentage of necessary awakenings
from sound sleep soon rose to 100%.

But then as so often happens, history repeats itself
and we begin to wonder what this work is coming to; for
as of now and forevermore we one-time babies, so rudely
awakened for devotions' sake now enthusiastically and
insistently proclaim that fathers should be so determined
that their children hear the Bible from infancy, they should
be awakened out of a sound sleep if necessary to hear all of
family devotions. "Train up a child in the way he should go
and when he is old he will not depart from it." "Seest thou
a man diligent in his business? he shall stand before kings;
he shall not stand before mean men."

As long as I live I'll never forget an experience we had in
Miami while visiting a Bible study group of about 100 people.

We had no part in the program but had been invited
by some friends to sit in on this class, which had a very
able and enthusiastic teacher of the Bible. By the time we
had arrived at the chapel building, the place was pretty
well filled and only a few vacant seats were left scattered
throughout the auditorium. Elisabeth and Dad sat up front

on the left, David sat up front on the right, Peter and I near the middle, and the rest of the family was scattered over the back section.

The Bible lesson started and the teacher was instructing all those with Bibles to turn to the various Scripture references that related to the subject.

I took notes on the whole lesson and as I counted later, the teacher used around forty different passages of Scripture from all over the Bible and had the audience turn to each one and read it aloud in unison.

One split second after the class was dismissed and the people had scarcely realized it was over, a man shot to his feet who had been sitting across the aisle from David and said in a clear voice everyone could understand, "Ladies and Gentlemen, I want you to know that there is someone in this audience that has done something which I didn't believe was possible. Here is a young man that, during this whole Bible study has quoted from memory every single passage of the Bible we have read together. He has not opened the Bible once and every verse was word perfect. I just think everybody should know about it." Another split second later a lady who was on her feet right beside David spoke out, "Yes, and if he hadn't told you about this I would have. I've heard about people that can do this, but I never thought I would get to meet one." Then leaning her neatly combed gray locks of hair down within two inches of David's neatly combed brown locks of hair and looking him square in the eye said with a mildly excited tone, "And what is your name son?" David, quite surprised by the whole affair, had his head bowed and raising it only slightly said in a low voice and with his face flushed, "David Pent."

From my vantage point in the middle of the auditorium it looked like the compliments and adulations were subsiding, but alas our host and hostess, sitting directly across the aisle from me were on their feet and said, "That's right, David can quote the whole New Testament and every other member of the family in proportion to their age can recite long passages of the Bible—in fact the rest of the family scattered all over this audience tonight never opened their Bibles either, and they travel around encouraging families to read the Bible together, and we surely should have them in our church for a program."

No experience David had while reciting in public was ever quite like this one. The setting was an invitation for us to perform at a large men's club and when we arrived, there were 300 men from every imaginable walk of life eating dinner together.

Their widely diversified business activities looked like two flies beside an aircraft carrier in comparison to the multitudinous of religions that they represented.

Our first song together was the Star Spangled Banner and as those 300 men stood and listened—"And thus be it ever when free men shall stand, between their loved homes and the wars desolation: Blest with victory and peace may the Heaven rescued land, Praise the power that has made and preserved us a nation, Then conquer we must, when our cause it is just, and this be our motto, in God is our trust: and the Star Spangled Banner in triumph shall wave, o'er the land of the free, and the home of the brave,"—the emotion and tears broke all over that great audience of men and we had their rapt attention from there on out to the end of our program.

The suspense came right near the end of the program when Dad introduced David's Scripture drama of Paul's Defense before King Agrippa from the 26th chapter of "The Acts of the Apostles" in the New Testament. Father explained by way of introduction, "Not long ago we were in Boston, Massachusetts, which is known for its great educational institutions. We were interested to read of a great conference of literary men who had gathered from all over the world to ascertain by mutual consent the greatest pieces of English literature in print. As one of the greatest, they cited Paul's Defense Before King Agrippa from Acts 26. David recited this passage not long ago in Ottawa, Ontario, Canada at the church where the Prime Minister attends.

"After his presentation, a leading attorney of Canada came to David and said, 'You know David, I've been making a thorough study of the great defense speeches of history and I think this 26th chapter of Acts is not only one of the greatest pieces of English literature in print, it's the greatest defense speech on record.' Well gentlemen, here it is, Paul's Defense Before King Agrippa. David, go ahead."

David stepped forward in his typical manner with hands behind his back and eyes firmly set as though in deep thought. After ten seconds of perfect silence he pierced the air with his oratorical style, "Then Agrippa said unto Paul, Thou art permitted to speak for thyself. Then Paul stretched forth the hand, and answered for himself: I think myself happy, king Agrippa, because I shall answer for myself this day before thee touching all the things whereof I am accused of the Jews."

As soon as he said the word "Jew" you could have heard a pin drop. At least one third of the men in this audience were Jewish. (Many Jewish people do not accept the validity of the New Testament canon and the fact that Jesus Christ came as the Messiah and Savior of the world. Consequently any reference to them in the New Testament is carefully scrutinized for accuracy in relation to its setting and connotations.) The Apostle Paul, a Jew himself, but a follower of Christ was defending himself and giving

90

testimony to the fact that Jesus Christ had changed his life.

David had reached the point in Paul's defense where he was relating his dramatic conversion on the road to Damascus with authority from the chief priest to persecute all the Christians. Here is a short dialogue:

"Which thing I also did in Jerusalem: and many of the saints did I shut up in prison, having received authority from the chief priests; and when they were put to death, I gave my voice against them. And I punished them oft in every synagogue, and compelled them to blaspheme; and being exceedingly mad against them, I persecuted them even unto strange cities.

Whereupon as I went to Damascus with authority and commission from the chief priests, At midday, O king, I saw in the way a light from heaven, above the brightness of the sun, shining round about me and them which journeyed with me. And when we were all fallen to the earth, I heard a voice speaking unto me, and saying in the Hebrew tongue, Saul, Saul, why persecutest thou me? it is hard for thee to kick against the pricks. And I said, Who art thou, Lord? And he said, I am Jesus whom thou persecutest. But rise, and stand upon thy feet: for I have appeared unto thee for this purpose, to make thee a minister and a witness both of these things which thou hast seen, and of those things in the which I will appear unto thee; Delivering thee from the people, and from the Gentiles, unto whom now I send thee, To open their eyes, and to turn them from darkness to light, and from the power of Satan unto God, that they may receive forgiveness of sins, and inheritance among them which are sanctified by faith that is in me. Whereupon, O king Agrippa, I was not disobedient unto the heavenly vision: But showed first unto them of Damascus, and at Jerusalem, and throughout all the coasts of Judea, and then to the Gentiles, that they should repent and turn to God, and do works meet for repentance. For these causes the Jews caught me in the temple, and went about to kill me."

As soon as David came to the phrase, "the Jews caught me in the temple and went about to kill me" there was a stir in the back of the auditorium and a Jewish man shot to his feet and

shouted vehemently, "You can't talk like that in here. I'm a Jew."

However, David continued in spite of the interruption trying to ignore the man. But he was insistent and vociferously said, "No, you can't talk like that here; this is a mixed audience and it's not fair." The audience was electrified and for a few seconds everybody, including David, seemed stunned. I didn't know on which side of the ledger public opinion was going to fall because of the large Jewish segment in the audience. Then everybody seemed to find their voices and at once started shouting and pointing, "Sit down, sit down, let's hear what he has to say. You can't disturb this whole audience." In fact some of his Jewish friends got so annoyed they walked right over to him, grabbed him by the shoulders, and sat him squarely in his chair.

This episode took about sixty seconds to transpire but seemed like sixty minutes. Anyway, it was long enough for large beads of perspiration to form on David's forehead, and little rivers started down both sides of his face.

The room was again in a hushed silence with every eye fixed on David, and he continued the story in spine tingling reality: "Having therefore obtained help of God, I continue unto this day, witnessing both to small and great, saying none other things than those which the prophets and Moses did say should come: That Christ should suffer, and that he should be the first that should rise from the dead, and should show light unto the people, and to the Gentiles."

As David concluded the story there was still a lot of pressure in the air—nothing audible but that awful sensation of—well, what's going to happen next?

Then Dad, displaying the best of his diplomatic strain and trying his best to see that all present got the right viewpoint said, "Now I don't particularly object to this man stating his opinion, however in this piece of literature we must realize that there were good Jews and bad Jews, good Gentiles and bad Gentiles. Paul himself was a Christian Jew and was relating how non Christian Jews were out to take his life.

"Of course, the main point of the whole passage was the conversion of Saul of Tarsus whose name soon changed to Paul the Apostle. If we will follow God as Paul followed Him, our lives will be productive and when we get to Heaven we will hear our Lord say, 'Well done, thou good and faithful servant.'

"I hope you gentlemen will take note of the main part of Paul's message: that Christ should suffer and die and rise from the dead and give new life and light to all who will believe and trust in Him for Eternal Salvation.

"Our only hope for peace with God is through our Lord Jesus Christ and if you will receive Him as your Savior from sin today, He will cleanse your life and make you His child."

9

Darling Dollar

The stare of lights from the oncoming cars seemed to never end as we pushed on into the night from a town in northern Mississippi. Our pocketbooks were completely empty and our stomachs weren't by any means overcrowded.

Fortunately, the cars were full of gas and we could reach the Mississippi town where a leading businessman had invited us to come sometime before. However, we had had no contact with him recently, and no programs or appearances had been definitely arranged.

We had no money to phone ahead to our friend, so because Dad definitely believed that the Lord was leading us there, we propped our eyes open for a seven-hour ride into the night.

On and on we drove past eleven P.M., twelve P.M., and up to one o'clock. By then we were all so sleepy we had to stop and catch a little snooze. But where were we to do a little thing like that in the swamplands of Mississippi?

A motel couldn't have possibly helped unless it was free, and that seemed unlikely, and the type of countryside we were driving through was inviting only for things like water moccasin snakes, cockroaches, and bony cypress trees.

Just as we were wondering where to rest ten sleepy people, our eyes discerned in the darkness a hundred feet ahead, a well planned picnic area with several cement picnic tables and benches.

As our wheels ground to a stop, Dad and I fell out onto a bench, pulling a blanket with us, and went immediately into a sound sleep. In twenty minutes we were ready and raring to go.

Now, I don't mean to be misleading in telling you we were raring to go in only twenty minutes, for you might think that a hard, damp, cement bench with a cool breeze is the answer to your sleepless nights. However, I will guarantee that if you were miles away from everywhere, lying out in the wide open nowhere, and you were to get a strong scent from a four legged animal with a white stripe down its back lurking near your resting place, you would be more than raring to go, tired or not. That pungent aroma from skunky kept us wide-awake four more hours

until we reached our destination.

We drove into town at six A.M. and wondered where in the world we would lay our weary heads. At this time of morning everybody was comfortably tucked in bed and we didn't have the heart to disturb them.

Believe me, we had plenty of nerves to disturb anybody; driving all night made them razor sharp, but our hearts got the upper hand this time.

Even though we scarcely knew a soul and had no promise of giving a program anywhere in town, Dad rented a room at a motel for $16 per night with two double beds and plenty of floor space. The total amount of cash between all ten of us was about $2.00. If the proprietor of the motel had known those facts, no doubt we would have concluded the evening on one of those sturdy Mississippi picnic benches. However, him not knowing, and us not worrying made for happy dealings and a worry free rest. He was resting on our word for his motel fee and we were resting on God's promise which states, "But my God shall supply all your needs according to his riches in glory by Christ Jesus." (Philippians 4:19)

After a good rest in the motel, we got up and all read the Bible silently for an hour before breakfast. You'd be surprised what that does for your mind when circumstances like this come along. We often think of the verse in First Peter 5:10 which states, "But the God of all grace, who hath called us unto his eternal glory by Christ Jesus, after that ye have suffered a while, make you perfect, establish, strengthen, settle you," and the Lord gives you perfect confidence and peace of mind that he will bring you through and you'll be better off when it's over.

Saturday morning we set out to contact our contact for an opportunity to serve the Lord on Sunday, and found that he was out of town.

After praying about this unexpected circumstance we decided to follow the exhortation, "Seek and ye shall find; knock, and it shall be opened unto you," and contacted the pastor of the man that we intended to contact first. The church was the largest in town and the pastor was a man of very definite convictions and rarely gave his pulpit to anyone else.

After talking with him and giving some samples of our testimony in song, he said that he would pray about giving us an opportunity to minister to his people the next day.

Sunday morning came, and we all dressed in our best bib and tucker and went to church. Evidently the Lord told the preacher the same thing he had indicated to us the day before, because that morning we had a wonderful time singing and giving the Word of God to a very receptive audience during the first half hour of the worship service.

After the meeting all the people came and thanked us for singing and giving Scripture presentations. However, when all the excitement had died away and the people had gone home, there we stood in the middle of the church with our hunger pangs trying to tell us how useless all that effort turned out to be. I'm thankful that hunger pangs and the things in the material realm don't serve as guideposts in the Christian's experience, because the Lord is perfectly aware of how we need food to keep going and certain material things to be efficient in His work.

We went back to our motel with mixed emotions over the morning's activities because we had all heard Dad telling himself, his family, and his audience how we had never gone without a meal. Every time a need came up the Lord would meet it.

The two dollars we came into town with had long since vanished and when one o'clock came, we were ten hungry people.

Since no one at the church invited us to dinner and we were penniless, I pretty well decided in my youthful mind that we just weren't going to eat this time. I got a blanket and went outside and lay down on the warm grass in the sun and asked the Lord to help us.

As I lay there and got hungrier and hungrier, I decided to take another look in my wallet just to make sure that there was nothing there. As I poked through some papers and my license I looked, and lo and behold, I found absolutely nothing there.

I settled back into the sun and tried to go to sleep. However, sleep would not come. Again I pulled out that wallet; this time taking every note and piece of paper and carefully unfolding and inspecting each item hoping to find some money. After combing practically every piece to the last business card, I had one big piece left to go—actually two pieces of paper stuck together. I carefully pulled them apart and peeked between and lo and behold, I found absolutely something there. That something was a one-dollar bill firmly sticking to the paper.

You can't imagine the excitement I felt at that moment. I ran in to tell the news to the rest of the family and found them praying and hunting for money too. They had come up with another fifty cents that we didn't dream we had.

The next question was what to do with the dollar and a half, now that we had it. We finally decided to try and find a grocery store that would be open and get as much as we could.

A committee of three was immediately dispatched for the job and came back ten minutes later with our "Sunday dinner." Everybody anxiously looked on as the contents were pulled from the bag. First, there was a quart of milk, then came one loaf of bread, then a jar of peanut butter and last of all a head of lettuce. David, being the exacting person in the family was given the job of dividing that quart of milk into ten glasses—evenly, and so with the rest of the food until each one had a fair share.

The next fifteen minutes, jaws moved in utmost silence as every mouthful was completely meditated upon and the greatest amount of food derived therefrom.

The amazing part about the whole thing is that after we were all through, we were as happily filled and content as if we had had a full course turkey dinner.

This was due, I believe, in a large part to our meditation on the Word of God. It is actually a fact from Christian medical men's viewpoints that the Bible nourishes your body as well as your soul. Solomon, the wisest man that ever lived, commenting on the Words of God, states in his book of Proverbs, "For they are life unto all that find them, and health to all their flesh." When you live God's way, He keeps you healthy.

If you want to save a lot of time, money, and anxious hours, get into the habit of waiting on the Lord by simply reading the Bible. It not only gives you a happier and more fruitful life, but in Eternity you will enjoy the benefits and reap the rewards of a righteous way of living. "Whatsoever a man soweth that shall he also reap" applies in part to being rewarded by God for your good deeds which are done on the positive and righteous side of God's ledger.

And don't be so concerned about material things, that you crowd God out, because as surely as you live to please him, those material needs and many times your material wants, He will abundantly supply. "Delight thyself also in the Lord; and he shall give thee the desires of thine heart." (Psalm 37:4)

The words of the Apostle Paul are excellent also: "I know both how to be abased, and I know how to abound:

everywhere and in all things I am instructed both to be full and to be hungry, both to abound and to suffer need. I can do all things through Christ which strengtheneth me." (Philippians 4:12,13)

There have been many times when we have had all that we needed ahead of time and we could see it all, and there will be more times like that. There have been many times when we didn't have all that we needed ahead of time and couldn't see any hope of obtaining it, but, "the Lord is faithful who has promised," and the need is always met one way or the other. As a matter of fact, you will find in your own experience that many times when you have seemingly nothing, you will be happier, because you are forced to lean on God's promises. The reason many of us are irritable and miserable, is simply because we have acquired for ourselves or are seeking to acquire a pile of this world's junk and can't see God for the pile, let alone realize how wonderful trusting God really is, and knowing the value of eternal life and the joys of Heaven. "If you know these things happy are ye if ye do them."

Now, getting back to the story we started. We had just finished "Sunday dinner" and it was drawing near the time of the evening services.

We prayed hard that afternoon that the Lord would work in the hearts of the people and that many would come to Him for salvation and re-dedication.

During the pre-service classes we were all scattered around the building in various classrooms giving our testimony and telling the people the value of the regular use of the Word of God in our lives, and trying to show them that they would greatly benefit by doing so also. A good verse for bringing out that thought and which we gave them is Joshua 1:8. "This book of the law shall not depart out of thy mouth; but thou shalt meditate therein day and night, that thou mayest observe to do according to all that is written therein… for then thou shalt have good success."

Next on the agenda was the evening service which we had full charge of, and gave a full program. The audience was deathly quiet, and no one moved for a solid hour.

At the close of the meeting, there was a great response to the invitation and many confessed Christ as Savior and hundreds of the congregation stood to their feet and made a solemn promise to God that they would spend time daily in the Word of God.

That night various people all over town invited us for a time of fellowship. One of them was the leading businessman who was head of the chemical industry in the city.

After it was all over we came back to the motel and learned that we were still as penniless as when we started out. We had one consolation: the pastor and our original contact who was back in town again had invited us to breakfast the next morning.

After breakfast the next day, the pastor gave us a check for seventy-five dollars.

10

Beans a la Lard

As we traveled through North Dakota we made sure to stop at a small town in central North Dakota where we had been invited by a friend to hold meetings.

As we rolled into the town late Saturday evening, we could see that the Indian tribe living on the reservation nearby had come to town for their usual Saturday night fling and things were really going strong.

A missionary who had worked there told us later that these same Indians still practiced the ancient dances of their fore-fathers, one of which is executed by tying a piece of rope to their ribs and then hooking the rope to a center pole. As they dance around the pole, they move farther and farther from it until their ribs become disconnected from their body. Also, since the white men have moved among them, they have acquired some additional tribal habits which their forefathers weren't able to do in their time, and that was stealing hubcaps and tires from people's cars.

However, we hadn't come there to tell them to stop doing such things as these; because drinking, dancing, and stealing are just natural tendencies of a sinful human being and showing them that these things were wrong was a complete waste of time at this point. We hadn't come to tell them what not to do; we had come with a positive plan, something which would change their basic and natural desires. After all, when you come down to the final analysis, people will do what they want to do, if they think they can get away with it. The Bible comments on this thought in Ecclesiastes 8:11, "Because sentence against an evil work is not executed speedily, therefore the heart of the sons of men is fully set in them to do evil."

We soon met our contacts who were the owners of the general store in town. They welcomed us warmly and told us that the store would close in a few minutes and they would direct us around to the various homes we would stay in for the night.

While waiting outside for directions, we couldn't help but notice a beautiful green hue to the evening sky. As we watched in amazement, the green hue grew stronger and darker until the whole sky looked like a sea of softly spun and tinted green cotton, gently moving with the breeze. It wasn't long before a dark strand of red wove its way from the northeast slowly making its way to the zenith of the sky. By this time other colors and shades began to appear such as blue and yellow, rolling and billowing with more and more intensity until soon you could not only see this magnificent sight, but hear it as well in the form of a crackling sound. The whole performance was so stunning that no one said a word for five minutes.

What we were watching is technically known as the Aurora Borealis, or commonly called the northern lights. It has not been positively determined what causes this phenomenon.

"The secret things belong unto the Lord our God: but those things which are revealed belong unto us and to our children for ever..." (Deuteronomy 29:29)

The Lord lets things like this stay unknown so that men will realize that God is still the ruler of the universe and holds the balance of power. "I am the Almighty God, walk before me and be thou perfect."

We were assigned to stay in three different places for the night with Dad, Ma, Peter and Tim going to a motel. Connie and Elisabeth went as guests of the family who owned the general store, and David, Paul, and I went out of town to be with a missionary family who were working with the Indians and also housing eight Indian orphans.

The next day plans were made for the meetings to be held and we were all excited and wondered what to expect from these people. A man had told us that as far as he knew, there was only one Christian in the whole town that really meant business and lived a life that proved it.

Some people who call themselves Christians aren't Christians at all. A Christian (or Christ one) is a person who trusts Jesus Christ as his personal Savior from sin, as it states in John 3:16, "For God so loved the world, that he gave his only begotten Son, that whosoever believeth in him should not perish, but have everlasting life." And the Apostle Paul further explains in Romans 10:9, "That if thou shalt confess with thy mouth the Lord Jesus, and shalt believe in thine heart that God hath raised him from the dead, thou shalt be saved." And, "Thou shalt call his name Jesus for he shall save his people from their sins." Also Romans 5:1, "Therefore being justified by faith, we have peace with God through our Lord Jesus Christ." This is what we would tell the people as they gathered to hear us in the meetings we had scheduled.

One was set for the mission church out of town and one was scheduled for the school auditorium in town.

The mission church meeting at the Indian reservation turned out as expected with a well-packed church and mostly filled with people who had been converted.

However, at the end of the meeting, there were several who accepted the gift of Eternal Life as offered in Romans 6:23, "For the wages of sin is death; but the gift of God is eternal life through Jesus Christ our Lord."

The meeting in town at the school on Thursday night came and we all piled into our old Desoto (the other two cars were stuck in the snow) and drove from the Quonset hut, which later had been offered to us for lodging, deep in the Indian reservation.

The dirt roads were very muddy that day and filled with holes. Each time we hit one, the poor old jalopy would groan under the weight of ten people in one car as the body would hit the frame with a resounding boom. The roads were already almost impassable as they were, but to top it all off, we heard on the radio as we drove to the meeting that there would be a heavy snow and ice storm in a few hours, which did not sound too pleasant for our trip back after the meeting. We arrived at the school thirty minutes before starting time but not a soul was there, not even the one that claimed to be a Christian. Ignoring the obvious fact that there would be very few attending, Dad set out to bring in more chairs and benches. "Come on you fellows," he said, mopping his brow, "help me get these benches set up for the people." We dragged our faithless feet into action and made ready for a crowd of two hundred.

Fifteen minutes before starting time, still no one had shown up; at ten minutes, still no sign of life; at five minutes we hadn't even scared up one Indian. The meeting was scheduled at 7:30 and as God is true, there was not one person there at 7:27—three minutes to go.

We had all just about figured on packing our gear and hitting the road, all that is except Dad. He was sitting over in a corner reading the Bible and praying, and trusting God to send some in. But most of us were thinking God would do well to consign them to their place of doom, because these people, white as well as Indian, just simply were not interested in hearing this Gospel and how they could be saved.

At 7:28 there was such a mad rush of people on that one little doorway that led to the auditorium that you'd have thought the world was coming to an end.

We never saw people come so fast and furious from nowhere in all our born days, and believe it or not, 7:30 found Dad hollering over the noise of the crowd, "Come on you fellows, help me get these benches set up for the people." By now our batteries of faith had been re-charged and David, Paul, and I started throwing benches around like porpoises throw balls at the Seaquarium.

At 7:35 the building was so jammed that we hardly had a place to stand for our singing and preaching.

There were white men, black men, and Indians filling the auditorium and all looking intently interested in what we were telling them about having peace in their heart and peace with God, freedom from troubles and fears, doubts and oppression. All this if they would have faith in God's plan of Salvation by trusting Jesus Christ as their Savior. Dad preached a fiery sermon that night and even though it wasn't very long (his sermons never were over 20 minutes), he said an awful lot and they just sat there dumbfounded at hearing such good news from the Bible.

Dad's sermons never were flowery or sermonic or oratorical. And here, as in many other places he simply quoted verse after convincing verse from the Bible, adding a comment here and there and then bringing it all to a head by toning down his voice and pulling out a dollar bill and saying, "How many of you children would like to have a dollar bill?" Invariably, several would raise their hands. "Well, I'd like to give this to the first one who will come and get it. But before I do, I'd like to give you just one more verse from the Bible. It says, 'For the wages of sin is death; but the gift of God is eternal life through Jesus Christ our Lord.' (Romans 6:23) Now, anybody who wants this dollar may come and get it."

The audience was electrified and not a soul budged.

"Now you see, I'm standing here trying to give away a dollar bill and nobody will come and get it. That's just what many people do when it comes to receiving eternal life. They say, 'It's all a joke,' or, 'It's too simple,' or 'It can't be true,' and because of their lack of simple faith, they put it off 'til later and many never give their hearts to Christ and end up in Hell forever.

Now I'm going to stand here until some boy or girl will come and get this dollar."

Most of the audience being country people and not used to being in crowds, made for an interesting sight from the platform. You could see little kids and big kids staring and gazing at that dollar bill, each one wishing to death that he could have it, but not having quite enough courage to walk up and get it.

Finally, after much coaxing and waiting, a little boy timidly walked up and took it. "Now," said my father, "if you'll just have as much faith in God as that little boy had in me, you can have eternal life right now! Jesus Christ died on the cross to save you and He rose again from the dead to show His power, and now He invites you to come to Him in child-like faith, not trusting in your little deeds and works, because God doesn't accept that. He said, 'For by grace are ye saved through faith; and that not of yourselves: it is the gift of God: not of works, lest any man should boast.' (Ephesians 2:8-9)

108

The only thing that would pay for our sin and let us go free was the blood of Christ, 'It is the blood that maketh atonement for the soul,' and since Christ was the only sinless man to live on the earth, only He could purchase this great gift for our redemption.

"What I would like to know and what the Lord is waiting to see, is how many of you people here tonight will accept the gift by believing on the Lord Jesus Christ."

There followed a deathly silence as battles were fought and victories won in the hearts of men and women, boys and girls. You could hear the clock ticking on the wall it was so quiet, and in fact with your eyes closed you could hardly tell that anybody was in the building.

Finally Dad said, "Alright, let's all look up this way. How many of you people in the audience took God at His word? In the Bible you know He said that, 'Whosoever therefore shall confess me before men, him will I confess also before my father which is in heaven.' The Lord wants you to have the courage to openly confess that you are trusting in Him."

This brought another electrifying silence and for a few seconds nothing happened. Then all of a sudden, hands began to go up as people got the courage and more would raise them and nod their head in the affirmative.

Shortly, scores of hands were in the air; varied in color in our eyes, but God wasn't looking at colors. He saw the honest hearts that were trusting and believing on Him.

Soon after this, the meeting was dismissed and the people vanished almost as quickly as they had appeared, but taking with them that basic ingredient for the power to change their lives and make them useful instead of wasteful and joyful instead of sinful. "If any man be in Christ, he is a new creature, old things are passed away behold, all things are become new."

Dad pulled away from the curb revving up the old overloaded Desoto and down the road we went, with our old chariot doing its dead level best to stay together. Every time the automatic gears shifted, there was a definite and unmistakable chewing and grinding of steel in the gearbox. However, as the saying goes, "When ignorance is bliss, 'tis folly to be wise." We didn't know what was happening under there but as long as the car kept going, that was all that mattered. A new gear system would cost more than the car was worth, so we decided to let her pick her time of quitting, and drive like nothing ever happened. And that's exactly how Dad drove it.

As we drove out of town, the roads were completely covered with a sheet of ice as slick as an ice skating rink and very dangerous. Having no chains on the tires and all those hills between us and our Quonset hut didn't help our frame of mind as we slowly crept along the slick highway.

We had been traveling for a half hour and each time we came to a hill it got more and more difficult to get over because of spinning wheels on the ice. Finally, we got to one hill and halfway to the top, the wheels started spinning and we were just barely holding our ground.

At this point there were two things we could do. We could either all jump out and push the car over the hill or let her coast back to the bottom and make a run for it. Just as we were wondering what would be best, Peter hollered, "Hey, Dad there's a light over there." Sure enough, as we stared through the snow we recognized the mission house cheerily lighted.

It was unanimously decided at this point to take advantage of the kind offer made to us and pile in for the night. Unanimously, that is, except for Ma. She contended that our hostess had enough to do to take care of her husband,

daughter and eight Indian orphans, without ten more piling
in. However, she couldn't rally enough support as we sat there
spinning our wheels on the ice, and the majority won.

Dad gradually let the car coast back down the hill and as
far up the next one as possible, so as to get into position for
the hot rod speed necessary to get up the hill and into the
driveway. There were two driveways: one for exit and one for
entrance, but the snow was so deep by now we couldn't tell
exactly where they were, so the car idled while each one tried
to recall where he remembered the driveway to be located
when he had been there a few days previous. David said he
thought it was over by that tree on the left side. Paul said,
"No, it's by that telephone pole," and I contended that the
two white posts marked either side of the passageway.

After a general forum on the subject, when everybody
had aired his views and Dad had decided where to head
for, he revved up Old Faithful again and made full speed
ahead for what we decided was the driveway.

Everybody closed his eyes as Dad leaned over like a
racecar driver and the car skidded around the corner. Sure

enough, and all to Dad's credit, we landed straight ahead and top side up in the very spot we had all decided upon. Yes sir, it was perfectly done and so well maneuvered only a ruler could have measured which was closest, the driveway to the right or the one to the left. Needless to say, we found the exact spot where the driveways weren't, and the ditch was deeper than it appeared.

The storm showed no sign of lessening, so the car was left embracing the ditch and everybody trudged through the snow for cover at the mission house.

For the next hour confusion reigned as eighteen human beings ran helter-skelter through a six-room house as suitcase after night bag, after cardboard box was brought into the hallway from the car.

The missionaries putting us up were very kind and worked hard to find room for us all.

I doubt if our hostess got very much sleep that night as she envisioned eighteen mouths wide open for breakfast and if the storm continued, for lunch and maybe on for the evening meal, making a total of 54 meals in one day. Also, she had made the mistake of telling our two girls, Connie, and Elisabeth to sleep in the same room with the four Indian girls and even though they were all happy about the whole affair, their happiness carried us on through the night 'till two A.M. when the hostess and guests took measures to convert the happiness into silence.

As the night passed, the storm developed into a full-scale blizzard and around 3 A.M. the telephone and all power lines—our only link with the outside world—snapped under the strain of ice, snow, and wind.

As morning came and the penetrating cold crept under our blankets, everybody got up to find out where the heat had disappeared.

Much to each one's dismay and consternation, as one by one they came into the furnace room, they found that the furnace was as cool as a cucumber and all electricity was off.

When the power lines had gone down, we not only lost contact with the outside world, but it so happened that the furnace was electrically controlled and so was the water pump and the stove. No heat, no running water, no cooking, and town was a real healthy ten country miles away.

The next thing to do, of course, was to get a fire going somewhere, somehow. That is, it would be the next thing for any average person, but since Dad wasn't average, building a fire wasn't the next thing that was done.

All our lives and most of his, he firmly and without deviation held to the rule of reading the Bible one hour before breakfast. As we were born one by one, instead of preaching its advantages and spiritual benefits to us and then letting us make our own decision, he simply told us to read it and told us how much to read it.

We will thank Father and Mother for persevering with us and making us do it. In fact, we will not only thank them all our days on earth, but if people thank people in Heaven, we'll probably thank them throughout eternity. It wasn't through philosophy, or psychology or psychoanalysis that we really learned to live and know God, it was the Bible read plain and simply without comment, at regular times everyday.

So, the first thing Dad did there in North Dakota was to read the Bible for an hour. However, under these circumstances he decided that two things could be done at once without losing too much efficiency and as various ones entered the furnace room to get a trace of warmth, he would set them reading to him and in half an hour after much blowing, shaking, and coaxing, his efforts of fire building were starting to be rewarded by a warm glow and

crackling in the coals. As soon as that magic word HEAT was passed among the other strandees, they all made their way into the furnace room and Dad had plenty of Bible readers for his last half hour of devotions.

After our stomachs had thawed out, we realized we were hungry. Our hostess informed us that she had twenty raw eggs and two glass jars of cold baked beans, which didn't sound like the most tempting delicacy or complimentary combination, but it was food and whether cooked or uncooked it was bound to be filling.

It was amazing though how our hunger pangs began to vanish into thin air as we savored eating cold baked beans and getting nourishment through a raw egg.

Just then our host came in from his hunting and proudly displayed a lard can he said would be a perfect container for cooking beans and eggs over the furnace fire.

He had tried his best to clean out the lard, but due to the cold weather, he had been only partially successful.

Lard or no lard, in went the beans, and the can was

114

suspended over the fire with the poker and shortly there were beans for all—a la lard. Then, in went the eggs for boiling, and another short period elapsed with boiled eggs for all—a la bean. Then the coffee went in and after another short period of time brought forth coffee for all—a la all the a las put together, and making a mighty powerful drink. Stormy morning turned to stormy afternoon, and stormy afternoon into stormy night with the situation growing no better.

Nothing could be done about getting food in, because the roads were impassable and the phone was disconnected because of power line failure.

Actually, to be completely factual, the roads were not as impassable as the cars were impossible. We owned three post war cars and the missionary owned one just a little more modern, but it ran worse than all three of ours put together.

The next morning the thick clouds showed their presence in massive gray fury as they rolled through threateningly.

Inside the six-room house, eighteen people ran hither and thither, jumping and slapping their hands to keep warm.

For two days we ate real cool food in a real cool house and generally speaking had a real cool time.

On the second day, Dad was determined to leave because we had an engagement several hundred miles away the next day and he didn't like the progress we were making to be at the meeting on time.

To complicate matters, two fresh inches of snow had just fallen the night before on the solidly icy roads and made things all the more treacherous.

But before anything was going to leave this mission those four cars had to be started, and you know we didn't just go out, turn on the key and drive off.

The Desoto was the best of the three and started right up, so fortunately we had something to work with.

With the Desoto and a rope, David and Dad proceeded to pull the old Buick up and down the icy road trying to get it started. They would no sooner get it rolling at the necessary speed when they were forced to jam on the brakes due to a sharp curve in the road. Then since there was a very steep hill beyond the curve they had to turn the cars around, (pushing the Buick by hand) and pull it the other direction.

It only took five men one hour to get it started and that after miles of slipping, skidding, and sliding.

This made two cars started and just two more to go: the last one of ours, and one of the missionaries who would escort us down the road several miles.

It was past noon when everything was percolating and babies and baggage were loaded for the trip.

Fortunately, a snow plow had been able to get through for the first time since our arrival just before we left, which gave us clear sailing ten miles into town.

After we had gassed up all three cars and in the process made our intentions known to the men at the station, the manager came to Dad with a very serious look on his face and said, "I strongly advise you to stay here tonight, especially with all those children. The forecast is for another blizzard in about thirty minutes."

Dad looked straight into the man's eyes and saw that he meant every word of what he said. But he never took anybody's advice before first asking the Lord what to do. So before making his final decision he asked the Lord whether it was yes or no, and we all prayed together.

Fact of the matter was, it was almost an impossibility as it was now to get over the plains country forty more miles to the next town. The snow plows hadn't even come through yet, and with three old cars rolling on twelve smooth tires and only one pair of chains, plus another

blizzard coming up, it looked like folly to try.

The missionary pleaded with us not to attempt it, the gas station men told us, "Don't dare try," and now the man recently come in from the snow plow said with a tone of finality, "It's impossible to make it to the next town."

I guess you know what happened next. Since God delights to do the impossible as He did with Moses and the children of Israel crossing the red sea, Joshua and the walls of Jericho falling down, and many others, He gave Dad a "yes" answer to that prayer back there, and now there was nothing, absolutely nothing that could hold him back.

We tore out of the gas station like speedsters in the Indianapolis "500" and started over the open plains.

There were over six inches of snow on the road and if the weather held clear, though it was slippery, we could see it wouldn't be too bad. However, in fifteen minutes there was such a snowstorm raging we could scarcely see the car ahead, much less the shoulder of the road.

Dad had the lead car with the chains making traction, David drove the middle car, and I had the wheel of the Buick bringing up the rear.

The storm was not only growing more fearsome by

the minute, but to add to the dilemma, some college boys came from behind in a sporty car and went speeding past our three cars. Five minutes later we found them around a corner with their car sitting sideways sprawled across the middle of the road stuck in the snow.

There again was nothing to do but stop and help them get going again, which we did. However, theirs was a light car with heavy chains and it wasn't much trouble for them to stop and go, but with us it was a different story.

When we were ready to go, the two rear cars did nothing but stand still and spin smooth tires on the ice.

We had with us one shovel and a chain four feet long, so Dad took the chain and hooked his car with David's car, the second in line, while I dug away the ice from the road, to get a running start and gain momentum from the rear. At Dad's signal while all the cars were touching bumpers and either pushing or pulling, we put the gas pedals to the floor and gradually began to move out.

The storm continued to increase until at one point out in the middle of the prairie, each car was on its own. Though we were each keeping a distance of only a few feet from each other, we could not even see the car in front of us, nor the shoulder of the road, and in fact we could hardly see to the front of the car the wind was so fiercely blowing the snow across the road.

Each carload was praying hard for guidance, and not just general guidance either, like some people say, "Lord, help us and guide us today, and thank you for everything." We could see absolutely nothing and it was the mercy of God that all three cars stayed on the road and kept moving.

When we got into the small town at nightfall, there were two small beds left in the hotel in town, and we slept on them, around them and under them.

The next morning a national guardsman told Father, "You were the last ones to make it in. We had to rescue several carloads during the night who ended up in the ditch." (It pays to follow the Lord's leading. "I will instruct thee and teach thee in the way that thou shalt go, I will guide thee with mine eye upon thee." In our experience during this time, this Bible promise was tried and proven.)

Even though our tribe of ten had gotten over the plains country, we still had by no means reached our objective. The day before we had only made it forty miles, which left over 200 miles to go to get to Fargo, North Dakota where we were scheduled in a Lutheran church.

Eight o'clock the next morning after each one had had his hour of private Bible reading and prayer, we all pitched in to get the cars packed and started. Eleven o'clock found one car started and the other two in a garage being dried out. The snow had blown under the hoods and into the motor and nothing would start until all the water had been dried from distributors, plugs, etc.

At twelve o'clock we rolled out of town to hit the main highway for Fargo. At the edge of town we saw cars lined up for several blocks and all traffic stopped. Dad went to inquire of the police officer about the cause of the tie-up, who replied in gruff and unyielding tones that no cars or trucks were getting past him until the snow plows and the National Guard came through from the next town. He added that there was not only too much snow on the road for traveling, but that 100 cars and trucks were stranded along the way; some in ditches, some right in the middle of the highway, some right side up, some sideways and some upside down.

When Dad asked when we would be allowed to proceed, he said, "Not sure, maybe three or four P.M."

Seeing that we wouldn't be able to get past him by

talking, Dad called us all together for a short prayer meeting. We asked the Lord if it was His will to get to our appointment that night, to somehow open the way for us.

Dad waited a few minutes and then spoke to the burly cop again, telling him that we had to be in Fargo at 7:30 P.M. for a preaching appointment and said that we would take the chance of being stranded if he would let us go.

He looked back at Dad with his chin set and eyes glaring and said, "Listen, here Mack, I told you once and I'm telling you again that nobody, and that means nobody like you or the next guy or the next, gets by here until that snow plow gets here. Besides," he continued, building up to a loud bark, "who do you think you are trying to get through here when all these hundreds of people have been sitting patiently waiting for hours ahead of you?" "Well," Dad replied, "that's fine, let them go if they want to and we can bring up the rear."

"Sorry," he said, "it's just plain impossible."

It was getting past dinner time so while the policeman was cooling down, we decided to go back into town and have dinner. After dinner came devotions and then another prayer meeting with words to the Lord not necessarily any more sincere than before but a lot more urgent and thoughtful. (We were all learning that God had stated certain things in the Bible which promised certain blessings if we would just make the request. So I guess everybody figured this was as good a time as any to see if they really worked. Consequently, it wasn't surprising to hear various members of the family praying such Bible quotations as: "If you ask anything in my name, I will do it;" "Ask and it shall be given you." "Whatsoever ye ask in prayer, believing, ye shall receive." Etc.)

All the time we had been away, cars and trucks had been

adding to the already long line of impatient waiters. Instead of pulling up in the back of the line like everybody else, Dad led his three-car caravan down to the left side of the road and pulled to a stop right under the policeman's nose.

As Dad got out to make a final plea for passage, the man eyed every move with a caustic but silent gaze.

Instead of asking anything, Dad just sidled up to him and started talking about the weather. "Well, I'm sure glad the sky cleared off," said Dad cheerfully. "Yup," said he, "yup, so am I." "Say," said Dad, "it must be quite a job to hold all these people here and still stay pleasant and civil."

"Yup," said he thoughtfully, "yup, you know a lot of people think I'm trying to be tough, but I'm just doing this for their good." "Yup," said Dad, catching the mood, "yup, that's right."

"By the way," said Dad (now that they were yupping in the same direction), "a few minutes ago one car came through Fargo, which must mean it's slightly possible to make it if we're careful." "No sir," said he, "you're staying put right here, yup, and nobody's moving until that snow plow gets here." Then talking out loud but more to himself than to Dad he muttered, "That snow plow sure is taking a mighty long time." "Yup," said Dad, "a mighty long time. What do you say," Dad continued, "we make a run for it? We just barely have time now to make our engagement. We'll be very careful and I'm sure God will enable us to get through."

"Well," he said thoughtfully, "so you think you can make it eh?" Then lowering his voice and turning on a slight grin he said, "Yup, O.K. you can try it."

That was all Dad needed and after giving one more "Yup" for good measure, he turned toward us, gave the familiar signal for starting up, jumped into the lead driver seat and we were off.

Even though the weather had cleared, the snow was still

very deep and we had to make our own tracks through it.

As Charlotte turned around to take a peek out of the back window she said, "Hey Daddy, all those trucks and people and things are following us." And sure enough, as we turned to look behind, there were tons of heavy trucks that evidently weren't going to let us go and have the cop make them sit there and wait.

Instead of trying to be the heroes and making the first tracks over this field of snow and avoiding the very possible possibility of getting stuck due to lack of chains, we let two or three of those big twenty-five ton semi trucks ahead of us, who made the finest path you could wish for and we sailed right on through behind them.

As we progressed through the afternoon, we could see more clearly why the police hesitated to let us proceed, because for miles and miles there were cars and trucks turned over in ditches, stranded along the highway, and you could see where many simply had to grind to a halt during the storm because the snow had engulfed their cars.

It is interesting to us as we travel to see how the Lord controls the weather and circumstances and how He so wonderfully helps those who put their trust in Him.

During the time when Joshua and the Israelites were fighting for the Promised Land, the Bible records that when they were being beset and troubled by their enemies during a battle that raged, and right at the time when things looked the darkest, it says, "There were more enemies killed by hailstones than the children of Israel killed with the sword."

Evidently the Lord directed each individual hailstone right where He wanted it and killed the enemies, and the Israelites not only won the battle, but saw with their own eyes how wonderfully God could work.

122

We often think, and you probably do too, when you seem to be surrounded with impossible circumstances and your enemies seem to have control of the situation that God isn't helping you like He promised He'd do. However, we must remember that if we don't have any battles, there won't be any victories.

The Word of God is as un-erring as it ever was when it states such encouraging promises as: "When the enemy comes in like a flood, the Spirit of the Lord shall raise up a standard against him." Also, "Call unto me and I will answer thee and show thee great and mighty things which thou knowest not," and, "God is my refuge and strength, a very present help in trouble, therefore will not we fear though the earth be moved and the mountain be cast into the depths of the sea."

Believe it or not, we reached Fargo and rolled into the church parking lot three minutes before starting time. To be perfectly honest, we were an unmistakable mess. Our shoes were scuffed and muddy from digging cars out of the snow, the girls dresses were so wrinkled that from a mile away you could tell they were from pure bred "missionary barrel" stock. As for the boys, we looked like loggers fresh out of the mountains with our tussled hair, and pants that looked like bent stovepipes.

Rushing into the church basement to clean up, Father hurriedly said, "Connie, clean up Charlotte, Arnold, clean up Timothy and Paul, and see that Peter looks neat. Everybody, be on the platform in three minutes."

Three minutes of washing, combing and grooming took care of us from the top of our heads to our waist, and then Dad told us all to get upstairs for the start of the program. After a few protests, especially from the female sector, we marched up to the platform hoping the crowded auditorium would understand the situation.

When we arrived, much to our delight and surprise, a missionary had just been speaking and the whole front of the platform (all the way from our feet up to our waist) was covered with maps and charts of his mission field. So confidently standing behind them, we sang and presented our program, and the audience never knew the difference.

11

The Floor Show

I remember being invited to sing on the floorshow of one of the most elite hotels in Palm Springs, California, the city that is famed as the vacation spot for movie, T.V., and Hollywood stars.

It was a typically hot Sunday morning in Palm Springs when the whole family gave a program at a leading church in the community and the Emcee for the floorshow was attending the service.

After our program, he came up and started talking with Dad, wondering out loud if we would be willing to make an appearance that afternoon about the middle of his show. My father replied, "Why sure, we go wherever we are invited and will be happy to be there."

Being an establishment catering strictly to high society, we were not sure exactly what the show involved, and that tingling sensation of entering the unknown gripped each one as our two cars drove through the exclusive arched entranceway.

As the caravan rolled slowly and softly past extravagant fountains and landscaping, David suddenly said, "Hey everybody, look over there, that banner over the arch—it says 'Big Bavarian Beer Festival.' Interesting we should be invited to a place like this."

Connie, with a sudden burst of bewilderment and then

letting her voice trail off said, "I don't know… boy, I can just see us now, singing hymns and quoting Scripture while they drink beer and drag on cigarettes. I doubt if we'll last very long here," and Ma sitting next to her and starting to fidget nervously said with trembling lips, "Whenever I get into situations like this, my knees just feel like water and I wish I could be back teaching the children their arithmetic or something."

I also was not without my tremblings, because, being from a family of total abstainers, you naturally get a funny feeling when malt, hops, and barley are the order of the day.

I can remember entering the dining area through clouds of cigarette smoke, seeing hundreds of people talking and laughing over their food and drink. The lavish drapes, thick carpets, and hanging chandeliers all were given special enchantment and elegance, as soft lights and mood music lazily entwined each other on the downy wings of balmy breezes. We were led through all this and past neatly uniformed waiters to a special table near the stage and given tickets for the Smorgasbord dinner.

The first concern of the waiter was how many drinks he should serve (and being a beer festival, we knew he wasn't referring to tomato juice). Dad didn't bat an eyelash

and replied "Ten." The waiter looked down the table
at all us little innocents and raising his eyebrows rather
unbelievingly, questioned, "Ten sir?" "Yes," replied Father,
"we'd like ten glasses of milk." The waiter again raising
the eyebrows in a new dawn of unbelief said weakly, "Ten
milks, sir?" "Yes, thanks," replied Father.

During the fine meal that was provided, entertainment
in the form of a jazz band and vocalists performed to
the crowded dining hall and bar. The bar was part of the
dining area but in relation to the stage was set all the way
in the back. A general din pervaded the whole area as each
entertainer executed his "show."

Then the emcee stood to his feet and said, "Ladies and
Gentlemen, we have a special treat for you today. Dr. and
Mrs. Arnold Pent and their eight children from Florida are
going to give us a show."

As we all climbed the stairs to the stage one by one
with knees shaking and nervous smiles, there was a definite
change in the mood of the audience...all the waiters
stopped, the cigarette girls stood still, the clatter of dishes
and eating faded, and even the men back on the bar stools
wheeled around to see what was happening.

By the time we were in formation on stage, the whole
place was deathly silent and lazy columns of cigarette
smoke drifted to the ceiling as a haunting reminder that
the people were all there waiting curiously at this sight of a
father, mother, and eight children on their floor show.

The silent stillness was electrifying as we looked out
upon these hundreds of people and they looked back at us,
wondering what to expect next.

Father stepped to the microphone confidently and
pierced the silence with these words of experienced
authority; "Ladies and Gentlemen, we're just here to tell

you what the Lord can do for a family. We like good times just as you do and we have found that Jesus Christ satisfies our hearts down inside where we all need satisfaction, and we have put our faith in Him. If you trust Him you will find the same satisfaction we have found and will be able to say along with the Psalmist David, 'He satisfies the longing soul and fills the hungry soul with goodness.'

"In almost a million miles of travel now, while this family has been growing up we have learned many songs and stories from the Bible, a few of which we would like to share with you. We'll sing for our first song, 'How Great Thou Art.'"

The audience remained very attentive. In fact their mouths just dropped wide open, so we put in everything they could take.

At the conclusion of the first song, after hitting the high crescendo and finishing triumphantly with Father taking the lead in a very clear tone, David and Paul giving a solid foundation of bass notes, Connie and Liz adding the subtle sweetness that altos bring, yours truly proclaiming the tenor, and Mother finishing with a flurry on the piano, suddenly we were through.

For a few tense seconds an overpowering silence prevailed, sending waves of unexplainable pressure that threatened to knock me off my feet. The clock ticking on the wall sounded more like the blacksmith banging his anvil, and beads of perspiration rolling down our faces added to the agony of the moment. Then like a wind rushing through the canyon, wave after wave of deafening applause shattered the stillness, and all we could do was stand there and smile, thanking the Lord for giving us this privilege of honoring His name.

The song we had just sung had a great message and it had gotten to the hearts of these hundreds of people; "And

when I think that God His Son not sparing, sent Him to die,
I scarce can take it in, that on the cross my burden gladly
bearing, He bled and died to take away my sin. Then sings
my soul, my Savior God to Thee, how great Thou art…"

The greatest thrill to me beside the actual truth of the
words was that those people out there, that I was so scared
of, were accepting that truth. It's something I hadn't dared
hope for at a beer festival.

After employing several other musical combinations
such as our Quintet, mixed quartet, and mixed trio, all
with equally enthusiastic response, Father decided to tell
them how it all started and why we were here. "You know,"
he said, putting one hand in his coat pocket and standing
casually, "it's interesting how we all got started in this job
of spreading the Gospel as a family and traveling constantly
as we do. My father was a cigar manufacturer from
Philadelphia and didn't know one verse of the Bible until
he was forty-five years old. He had three cigar stores in the
city and was starting to make a real success of his business
when Billy Sunday, the great Evangelist of the 1900's,
came to town. He wasn't the lest bit interested in what
Billy Sunday had to say and never even went near the big
tabernacle that was packed with 25,000 people every night
to listen to the Gospel. But then one day, some young
fellows came to Juniper and Sansom Street, where one of
his cigar stores was located, and held a street meeting. Not
even caring to hear them, he went about his business inside
the store. However, the fellows were preaching pretty loud
and he couldn't help but hear one, especially when he said,
'For God so loved the world, that he gave his only begotten
son; that whosoever believeth in Him should not perish,
but have everlasting life.' This verse (John 3:16) really
made a lasting impression on him and when he got home

he got a Bible and started reading. It was just a few days later he told Mother, 'You know, since I've started reading this book and put my trust in the Lord, I have peace in my heart. Let's read this book together every day.' The outcome of this Bible reading was that he put his trust in Jesus Christ as his Savior, quit the tobacco business, and studied for the ministry at the age of forty-five.

"Well that caused quite a stir in the family circle, and it was hard for some of his relatives to accept such sudden change. His brother Howard came to him one day and said, 'Arnold, you better think of your responsibilities. You've got two boys in college and a family to support, and you don't know a thing about preaching. Here you're leaving a business you've been building up for 25 years and made a success at, and now you say you're going out to preach the Gospel. How are you going to support your family?' 'Well Howard, I read in the Bible where it says, 'Seek ye first the kingdom of God and his righteousness,

and all these things shall be added unto you.' I believe
I've got a God that I can trust and I'm going to have
the satisfaction of trusting Him this once. My business
associates don't know any more about God and the Bible
than I did and I'm going out to teach them.'

"It was Saturday when he made that decision and on
Monday he was completely out of the cigar business.

"Now just to show you that God never lets us down
and keeps His promises, you should know this. My
father, after leaving the tobacco business, went into the
electrical business on the side as he studied at nights for
the ministry. He was soon making more money on the
side selling washing machines and vacuum cleaners than
he did when he was the head of the firm of Pent Brothers
Cigar Manufacturers. You see, it's true, "Seek ye first the
kingdom of God and his righteousness and all these things
shall be added unto you."

"This great change that came over my father was not
that he was embracing a new code of ethics or changing
his religion. He believed on Jesus Christ as his Savior and
trusted His promises in the Bible; that's when the big
change came. You see, the Scriptures say, 'If any man be
in Christ, he is a new creation, old things are passed away,
behold all things are become new.'

"When we give Christ our lives, He gives us a new life.
We are actually "born again"—spiritually.

"When all these young people of mine were growing
up, we taught them the Bible and showed them how to
give Jesus their hearts at a very early age and that is why
they are on the road today traveling thousands of miles
every year, encouraging others to do the same.

"You see, Christianity is simply a person. It's 'Christ
in you—the hope of glory.' It is the most revolutionary

experience a person can have. It will change your whole
life. It will give you purpose and direction and peace and
joy and the promise of Everlasting life. Jesus said, 'I am
come that they might have life and that they might have
it more abundantly.' If you want an abundant life and one
that will please God here and make your life worth living
and give you something you would be glad to die for if
necessary, then I urge you to take God at His Word and
put your faith and hope in Jesus Christ as your Savior from
sin which has condemned us to eternal death."

At this point, as through the whole message, the rapt
attention of every last person was overwhelming and at
the conclusion of this part of the program (I don't think
the emcee had put on all the talent for the day) they all
came surging to the front by the stage, asking counsel on
spiritual problems and wondering how we ever did what
we were doing as a family. If the emcee hadn't planned on
closing at this point he soon made up his mind because all
interest for the floorshow had vanished.

Yes, we were still at the beer festival, and it was
even more than I ever dreamed could happen. What
an unexpected experience. And yet why should I be so
surprised? Why shouldn't I expect it? After all, isn't this
the greatest experience that can happen in a person's life?
Why shouldn't they accept it? (Can you think of one valid
reason why a person should not want Jesus Christ as Lord
of their lives?) They were human beings with problems,
and cravings and longings for reality. Here I was only
sixteen and I actually had more peace and joy than most
of them ever thought of having. Jesus Christ had given me
joy and peace even beyond my fondest hopes. Many of
these people by their own testimony were miserable and
dissatisfied. I stood near the stage and heard with my own

ears, voices high on the social ladder painting the picture of
life in the dullest and dreariest of oils.

A lady I overheard talking to my mother nearby—I
couldn't help but look at her as she came and grasped
my mother's hand in both of hers and said with tears
in her eyes, "Mrs. Pent, I don't have a care in the world
financially, but this is what I need. I want you to remember
me in your prayers," then handed her a contribution to
help in our expenses.

This experience turned out to be a time of strengthening,
not only for those that heard the Gospel through us, but for
us, Mother included, and this is the thing we need, because
Jesus Christ came into the world to save sinners, and saves
to the uttermost all who come in simple faith to the Lamb
of God who takes away the sin of the world.

Just as a sidelight, there are some people who never get
the point, and you can explain the Christian life and tell
how to be saved from eternal death and enthusiastically
explain all the joys of walking with God, but they just
look at you real thickly and it doesn't seem to sink in.
There were at least two men there that day in this category
because I overheard them discussing the program. "You
know, that sure was a fascinating family wasn't it?" said
one. The other replied, "Yes it certainly was. I wonder how
they get their education? I don't see how they could do it
being on the road all the time." "You know Harry," said the
first, "that program they gave was o.k. but the music, well,
it just didn't have the beat that we usually get when we come
here. Most of the time, at least if it doesn't beat it will have
a good swing to it." But that, too, was the providence of God.

Anyway, for every two that missed the point that day
there were at least twenty-two who got it and they were the
ones we were interested in.

12

Home Education
Kindergarten to College

I can remember the day Father made the decision to keep us out of public school. David was just entering the 10th grade, Connie was starting in the 9th, I was preparing for the 7th, Elisabeth was going into the 6th, and Paul into 5th. Peter, Timothy, and Charlotte were all pre-school age.

We had just returned to Florida from the state of Maine, where we operated a summer Bible conference.

Father was driving down Lake Underhill Drive in Orlando, Florida, and we were all in the car together. Mother said rather casually as she sat beside him, "Well, Arnold, when shall we put the children back in school? They ought to be put in pretty soon so they don't get behind."

There was a moment of silence and Dad said thoughtfully, "I don't think the Lord would have us put them in school this year." To which mother replied in a worried tone, "Well, how can they ever get a decent education without going to school?"

"That is something the Lord will have to help us with," he replied, "But I just don't think it's right to let an atheist or non-believer have our children the best part of every day, teaching them many things that we will have to turn right around and tell them are not true."

That was all that was said in that conversation, and we

never studied in a classroom again.

The next day, Mother went to a bookstore and bought enough books to carry us all through the year.

Little did she realize back in her college days when she majored in teaching that God was preparing her to teach her own children.

She has said many times if she knew all the problems and hard times she would go through, she probably would have run away like Jonah did. But God gave her grace to live a day at a time and enabled her to do the job. Of course, now, she's so glad she did.

It was quite an adjustment at the beginning to study without the material we were used to at school, and I had a miserable time getting through the 7th grade. But our challenges as students were just a drop in the bucket compared to our dear mother, who was juggling teaching all these grades at once, housework, and the many activities in which we found ourselves.

Of course, Father's stand in this schooling matter was not very well understood by the authorities for a while. The school board didn't even realize we were out of school for about six months because we were always gone half the year anyway, and they never knew when we came back from traveling somewhere. So when we didn't show up in school, nothing much happened for a while.

Then one day a truant officer came by the house and wanted to know why all these children were not in school. Fortunately, Father was home when she came by and we were all in our little nooks doing studies.

Father did not say a thing about not agreeing with the school board and how he thought it was a bad influence on his children. He knew full well she would have stalked out in a rage and messed the thing up for good.

The lady was a very typical "officer" type of individual and sat in the living room with a terse look as Father tried to explain. "You see, ma'am, we are on the road much of the school year in Evangelistic work and it would not be fair to the school system or these children to be pulling them out of this school and putting them in that one. However, we make sure they get all their studies in, and in addition they receive all the experiences that come from traveling. Then we appear on radio and T.V. programs and sing in churches and clubs, and this gives them a good practical education in things that really count. In addition to all this, they receive many hours of Bible reading each week and all these children can quote books of the Bible."

When Father had finished, the lady seemed a little bit more favorable, but she was not persuaded. She said the law was that children must be in school and, since we were legal residents of Florida, that law pertained to us unless we received some special permission.

When she left, Dad gathered us all in the living room and asked the Lord to work out the details and keep things under control. However, one thing was sure. We were not going back to school.

A few days later, a truant officer came by again with a message from her superiors. They requested Father's presence in their office.

When she left there was another prayer meeting in the living room, and you could feel a little more urgency among those that prayed.

The day came for the appointment and the Pent house all prayed as their leader went to see the authorities.

When Dad drove in the driveway after the meeting, we all ran out the back door hollering, "Daddy, what did they say? Are we going to get into trouble? What do we

have to do next?" But Dad had a lot on his mind and came walking in the house with a thoughtful look on his face and an armload of printed matter.

Everything was perfectly quiet except for a few nervous whispers among the smaller children as we all stood in the kitchen waiting anxiously for the latest news.

"Well," said Dad with a little sigh of exhaustion, "I had a good conference with the authorities, telling them about the same thing I told the truant officer. When I had finished, they said to me, 'Mr. Pent, you are giving your children far more than we can ever offer the average child in our schools. If your children will take these tests and pass satisfactorily, it will not only prove your point, but give us something to satisfy our superiors that they are being educated properly.'" Then Dad opened up the tests and told us to get to work.

We never heard another word from the truant officer or her superiors, so I guess our grades were satisfactory.

After struggling along for about a year in the trial and error method of teaching and learning, someone told

David about the American School Correspondence Course in Chicago, Illinois, which offered a complete high school education all by correspondence at a reasonable monthly rate.

In a short time, the whole Pent family was going to school by correspondence and Mother's burden was greatly relieved.

Studying by correspondence turned out to be exciting and we worked enthusiastically. When it came to speed on finishing, Paul took the cake, finishing the four year course in two years.

After getting everything straightened out with the Florida authorities, Father felt we should go to California and do evangelistic work there. So off we went taking everything, including our school.

There had been no advance arrangement out there or any itinerary made up except for one meeting in a small church way up in Northern California that had been arranged about six months previously.

After driving for thirty-five hundred miles from the East Coast to the West Coast, averaging over 500 miles a day, we arrived at the small church a day early.

Father went to introduce himself to the pastor and get acquainted a little better but the pastor didn't recognize him and when Father mentioned the special meetings he said, "What meetings?" And so it turned out that the church had changed pastors and the former pastor had forgotten to mention the date to the new preacher, nor had he notified us.

Since we had arrived a day early, the present pastor went to work on the telephone, the radio and every other means available and at 7:30 the next night, the house was packed and many professed to follow the Lord.

Even if the meeting had been cancelled, Father wouldn't have been greatly disturbed. God wanted him here and that was all he knew (except for the fact that

all the money had been spent and he didn't know how
he would be feeding 9 hungry mouths for the next few
months). But that never seemed to worry him. He just
quoted some Scripture, cited the unfailing promises of
God, and kept going.

During family devotions just before that first evening
meeting in California, Father said, "The Lord promises, 'I
will give you the treasures of darkness and hidden riches
of secret places' (Isaiah 45:3) and 'My God shall supply
all your needs according to his riches in Glory by Christ
Jesus,' (Phil. 4:19), so let's ask the Lord to give us faith to
believe it and the Lord can use us for His glory."

From that day on, invitations started coming in
and three months later as I looked at our schedule, we
had traveled thousands of miles, averaging almost two
programs every day with hundreds of professions to follow
Christ, capacity audiences, and enough money to meet our
needs. We finally settled down in Southern California and
got down to business on our schoolwork.

Everything was fine for six months and Peter, then six years
old, joined the ranks of the school age with Mother teaching
him from books she had purchased from a school supply store.

One night, Paul and I walked over to the school gym
where several boys were playing basketball.

As we walked up to make friends, they gave us the cold
shoulder and we had a rough time making their acquaintance.

Finally, one of the roughest of the group sauntered
over with his hands stuck half way in his pockets and
stood before Paul and me with his eyes half opened and
half closed. "Where are you fellows from anyway?" he
questioned gruffly.

Paul, who was about half the size of our opponent but
twice his size in determination, eased over until he was

right under his nose and putting his hands half way in his pockets and letting his eyes droop, looked up at him and said, "Oh, we don't know especially, we're really not from anywhere." That answer was exceedingly unpopular, and the toughie hollered over to ten or fifteen of his cronies, "Hey, fellows come 'ere a minute, we've got a real smart aleck here who needs to learn a few lessons." As those tough boys shuffled over to meet us, I could feel the blood rushing to my head and sweat running down my back. In a few seconds they were all looking down at us threateningly, but we stood our ground firmly and didn't bat an eyelash (we were really too scared to do anything).

One boy from the group volunteered a suggestion, "It wouldn't be very enjoyable for all of us to work them over at once. Why don't you take the smart aleck there, (pointing to Paul), and teach him alone. If you need any help just say the word, and we'll be ready." So the leader, taking off his shirt motioned to Paul, "Come on, let's have it out." But Paul was nowhere near as big as this delinquent, so I stepped up to him and said, "That's my

brother and you better just keep your hands off him. Why
don't you pick on somebody your own size? You're such
a coward, you probably wouldn't dare, and besides, all
you fellows must be awful hard up for something to do.
We came in here to make friends, not fight." But the last
sentence was lost in the confusion as 20 undisciplined,
wild boys pulled off their sneakers and started punching
and beating us over the head and chasing us up and down
the bleachers and over the gym floor.

After what seemed like an eternity of fright and our share
of bruises, the principal, who had been working late in his
office, came over to see what all the commotion was about.

As soon as his face appeared in the doorway you could
have heard a pin drop and his gruff voice echoed through
the gym, "What's going on in here?" Every head hung
except two, and we two walked out the door to safety.

Not thinking about the school situation, we accepted
the principal's offer to drive us home and he apologized
profusely on the way for the conduct of his boys.

As he started asking questions about who we were,
how long we had lived here, etc. we began to wish we were
still back at the gym being beat on by some more tough
guys because the answers weren't very easy to come by.

He dropped us off at the driveway, and we went in and
right to bed without saying anything to anybody about
what had happened.

The next morning about eight o'clock, the whole
family was sitting around the breakfast table when a knock
came at the front door. Paul and I couldn't have wanted a
hole in the floor any more than we wanted one right now.
It was the principal! Father didn't have the slightest idea
who he was and smiled him into the kitchen where six
school age and two pre-school age children were sitting

(sitting ducks). I don't need to say much more except that my father meant to keep us out of school and the principal and those at the local school office meant to put us in.

From that day on and for a long time after, Father was trying to fulfill this regulation and that law in between discussions with uncooperative truant officers.

Finally the pressure got so bad that one morning Dad made an announcement, "Everybody pack your bag, we're going to Sacramento, (the capitol of California) and get this thing settled once and for all." "But Arnold," Ma interjected with concern, "that's 500 miles up and 500 miles back. Why does everybody have to go?" "I don't care if I have to go 5,000 miles; these are my children and they'll be taught the way God wants them taught if I die in the attempt."

Sacramento didn't turn out to be much more cooperative, but they did reach an unsettled truce which hinged on Father and Mother obtaining transcripts from their college days (Mother from Wheelock in Boston, Massachusetts and Father from Wheaton in Illinois) proving their qualifications to teach grade school and high school.

After staying in Southern California longer than we had ever stayed in one place at one time, eight months, and encouraging and teaching many thousands of families all over that wide area to read the Bible and serve the Lord, Father felt the call again and we headed for still new adventures.

About twelve years after these experiences with school authorities, Father received an advantage he greatly deserved. After eighteen years of formal training himself, training eight children with Mother's help from kindergarten to college, he received recognition from the state of Florida to grant degrees for the study of the Bible and the Homestead College of Bible Correspondence Courses was born. Now people all over the country, for a very nominal charge, study the Bible and receive state recognized credit beside the particular advantage there is in just studying the Bible.

Seeing that many institutions were denying the authenticity of the Bible and many young people and older people as well were asking for good old-fashioned Bible study, our whole family is now heavily engaged in teaching the things we have learned from the Scriptures to people who study the lessons in their own homes.

Anyone who desires a good education can get it by studying the Bible as we have done, and the reports of progress in the lives of people we have never seen is tremendously encouraging.

13

Physical Fitness and Health

1 Timothy 4:8 tells how bodily exercise is profitable for the little time we are here on earth and that exercising ourselves unto Godliness is profitable not only for this life but the life to come.

Not only did Father see that we exercised ourselves in Spiritual activities, but he had very definite ideas and laws about keeping in good shape physically.

One time, driving peacefully along the highway on our way to another singing and speaking engagement, we were way out in the middle of nowhere and suddenly Dad pulled the lead car to the shoulder of the road and ordered everybody out. Then displaying his rigid military mood said, "We're going to take a half hour walk! If you like, you can walk ahead and we'll pick you up along the road, or you may take a stroll through the woods, but be sure you get at least thirty minutes of good exercise." Immediately there was an uproar. "But Dad, can't we walk when we get there?" says Elisabeth. "I don't feel like it!" says Connie. "Honestly, it seems as though we can't get 25 miles before we either stop at a fruit stand, take a walk, get gas, go to the bathroom, or something else" says Ma all in one big sigh. Of course this brought on a military type lecture from Dad, but five minutes later everything was back to abnormal and ten Pents were scattered over the Virginia countryside.

Four or five of us started walking down the highway at full speed. I'll admit it is a rather strange sight, especially when we get in expanses like New Mexico or over hill and dale like Virginia seeing a family walking at top speed when there isn't a house or town for miles.

Evidently people took pity, because more often than not people would stop and offer rides, but we just smiled pleasingly and said, "Oh no, thanks, we're just out for the exercise." Then not realizing we were connected with the cars a mile or so back they would look at each other quizzically, then look back at us skeptically, then look down the long road wearily, then look at us again over their layers of fat and shake their heads in wonderment. You don't lose much weight when you shake your head, but you do lose when you shake your hips with a good brisk walk.

One time a man in an old car and heavily laden with John Barley Corn stopped and asked, "Does ya need a lift?" Paul stepped up to the window and said, "No thanks, we're just walking for the ride."

Incidentally, it was just a matter of time before some of the loudest complainers in the family became the most avid supporters of good strenuous exercise, and walks were made the rule voluntarily. Nothing is thought of it now when the whole caravan pulls over on the shoulder of the road and everybody piles out for thirty minutes of exercise. On a long day's trip we take thirty minutes before noon and thirty minutes after noon.

The girls in our family were like very other girl when it came to dieting. They were forever buying books on subjects like, "Easy Method to a Perfect Figure," "Lose 10 Pounds in Ten Days" and the like, but for some reason never lost much weight. Then they decided they needed a scale, so they invested in some scales, but that didn't trim anybody down either. All it did was keep them up to date on how thin they weren't. One time they tried a super-duper egg and spinach diet for two weeks, eating only eggs and spinach, but all that produced was a firm distaste for eggs and spinach.

Then one day Dad encouraged them with a few subtle suggestions to take some good long walks and work off some of the expensive diet food they were buying and lose some weight.

So with encouragement from the male sector of the family, but mostly from their own initiative, they started a walking program. We were in Miami, Florida when they had been hiking at intervals for a couple of weeks and had built up some stamina. Starting from 107th St., they walked to the downtown Miami Post Office for a total of 102 blocks and back, then shortly after that strode six miles in another direction. The two interesting facts were that it wasn't necessary to recuperate for a week with aching limbs and stiff joints, and also, some of the diet food was beginning to wear away and the pounds started coming off.

When it comes to diligently sticking to a rigid discipline of exercising in our family, the one who takes the first prize is Paul (fifth from the oldest), and many of us follow his methods in varying degrees to keep in good condition.

Regular strenuous exercising is done no matter where we happen to be. Sometimes we shake the whole house where we are being entertained overnight, and many times those with whom we are staying join the fun.

One time in a crowded motel room, when we were in a hurry to get to a meeting and when everybody had finished his morning devotions, at once, without a word, Paul opened the motel door, stuck his legs and feet into the passageway, and went to town doing his sixty sit-ups.

Peter and Timothy started their first throws at the pictures on the wall, David warmed up with knee bends and the mirror, and the only place left for yours truly to do push-ups was to open the bathroom door and put half of me in one room and half in the other.

When this whole business got started it really wasn't safe for one to be around, unless one knew every act and how long it lasted, because flying fists and kicking feet were covering every square foot of space, and one was just liable to get some unexpected exercising in a place one didn't anticipate.

All of us boys started this exercising with about 25 sit-ups and 10 push-ups. As each one got older, he increased his quota until he got to 60 sit-ups and 50 to 60 push-ups. This is no Olympic record, but when you do this four days a week, you don't feel like breaking world records every day. If you will try this same method, you probably won't break any records either, but for a while you'll sure feel like a broken record.

Peter and Timothy, the two youngest boys, followed our example and started exercising at eight years old. After they got going, it wasn't unusual to have them doing 40 sit-ups and 30 push-ups each morning.

It was interesting to watch their red, flushing faces with every muscle taut and big gasps of air from numbers twenty-five through thirty. If you heard a heavy grunt, then a groan, then a big explosion of air, it meant they didn't quite make it to the top for the thirtieth.

When a person rides thousands of miles each year, as we do, and sits in meetings frequently, he either gets accustomed to it and puts on the pounds, or does regular exercise to keep in good shape.

Since many miles of riding has been and is part of our daily diet, Paul decided he would choose the "regular exercise to keep in shape" method for good health, and he really got

148

himself involved in a big way. In fact it wasn't long before I joined in with him, and we worked together on it.

I remember when we first started the idea of road running. We were at a motel in Corpus Christi, Texas, on the Gulf of Mexico.

After riding all day, we just couldn't wait to get out and do some strenuous exercising, so we just took off and ran down the highway at about ten o'clock at night. It felt so good and was so stimulating, we decided to make it a regular habit, and from then on until a year and a half later, we ran thirty minutes every day Monday through Friday. Then we discovered that our muscles were getting torn down, and that five days a week year round was a little too much. So we cut it to Monday through Thursday, and it worked out very well. After continuing this for over a year, we leveled running speed at about 9 miles an hour. On an average day we were able to make about 4 ½ miles in 30 minutes.

Our running route and terrain is different every week. Sometimes it is mountainous, sometimes flat. Also, we can't always run during the day when we most prefer to, because of too much work on radio or T.V. programs, or clubs or churches, so we have to hit the rail at night, which, instead of discouraging us or wearing us to a frazzle at the end of the day, serves to build us up even more and also turns out to be rather enchanting at times.

One time in Wisconsin during the fall of the year, it turned to pitch black at night by nine o'clock. It was almost black enough to feel. We were running through the countryside during this time and there wasn't a house or a car or anything to give light. We could not see where we were going, and in fact it was so black we could not see the edge of the road we were running on. The only way we knew whether we were going right was when we felt the grass on the shoulder of the road under our feet.

Other times during night runs, when we couldn't see much, it was comfortless to be able to smell something but not know where it was. One skunk got so near we could taste the smell in our mouth, and I think we must have done a world's record hundred-yard dash to clear the area.

We contend daily with the problem of competing with traffic and running under every condition imaginable. However, though we have not beat any world records yet, such activity does have a tendency to take out any restlessness one may possess.

Having the certain advantages of a nice high speed track to run around is almost unheard of in our experience, and besides, when you're running 5 miles and have only a quarter mile track it means that you must run completely around the track twenty times, and this is rather monotonous. I do remember one track we tried in Danville, Virginia, where we were having some meetings. We had just started and were on the second lap when a couple of fellows came and sat on the sidelines. A couple more laps around and three more fellows appeared. We didn't realize they were on the school track team and needed to work out, so we just kept on running around and around and around and around. It wasn't long before they got tired of this routine and joined in with us. As we went around together, they asked all kinds of questions wondering where we came from, who we were, and when we would be through. (We still had twenty minutes to go.) If there's anything I don't like to do when I'm running it's carry on a conversation. It's hard enough to get your breath as it is, and when the leader suggested we race around one time I gladly took him up on it. About halfway around, he pulled a ligament in his leg and went limping off, so

that took care of that. But about then, their school coach
was standing in the middle of the track waving us down
with a very angry look on his face. When we stopped, he
gave us the loudest, ugliest bawling out I ever heard. When
he finished we just stood there with our heads down and
didn't say a thing. This made him all the angrier, and he
told us to get out and never come back. When I saw he
was through I said, "Sir, we didn't realize these fellows were
on a track team and had no intention of upsetting your
schedule." We left promptly.

We much prefer fighting city traffic and climbing old-
fashioned country hills to running on prepared tracks. It
is very stimulating to the body and certainly does wonders
for one's outlook on life.

Many times I have started my 5 mile jaunt in a
complacent sort of way, maybe sometimes a little bored
with life, or even discouraged and disillusioned but after
this wonderfully exhilarating experience, I have come back
with fresh determination to go on in spite of difficulties.
There is no doubt about the fact that it greatly relieves the
tremendous pressures that we undergo in this world. But I
must stress here that no matter how strenuous the exercise
or satisfying the immediate results, the determination
to go on is spite of the difficulties will only come when
sufficient physical exercise is coupled with a heart to know
the God of the Bible and to desire His will for your life.
That's why the Apostle Paul said, "I beseech you therefore
brethren by the mercies of God that ye present your bodies
a living sacrifice, holy, acceptable unto God, which is your
reasonable service; and be not conformed to this world but
be ye transformed by the renewing of your mind, that ye
may prove what is that good, and acceptable and perfect
will of God."

Incidentally, if you are long on Bible study or too much office work and short on good physical exercise, your mind becomes clogged and you can neither study nor meditate efficiently. You must have a good balance.

From the majestic Canadian Rockies to the palm-lined avenues of Miami, we ran, seldom missing a day during the week, no matter how early or late we had to do it, or regardless of where that day, in God's providence, we found ourselves. And it was many a day we knew not where we would be twenty-four hours later.

In Montana, running near the Canadian line, the border patrol picked Paul and me up and accused us of coming across the lines and avoiding custom's officials. It was late in the afternoon, and we had just come down from the Canadian Rockies in Alberta and were greatly in need of some strenuous exercise. I can remember chugging up one of the longest hills we had ever tried to conquer and getting far enough over the top to really pick up some speed. Just as we were enjoying the advantage of all that momentum, with hair flopping and shirttails flapping, the patrolmen came beside us and signaled both of us to stop.

We usually get clad in fast clothes (sneakers, tee shirts, and running pants) but this day we were in such a hurry to run, we just jumped out of the car and took off in a mad scramble down the road in the slowest clothes we had, (heavy shoes, long pants, sport shirt, etc.), and as I think back, the way we were running down that hill, it sure must have looked as though we were running for something besides exercise.

When they asked for identification, we had none with us, and when Paul gave them the exercise line, they couldn't have looked with more accusing unbelief. However, as the body heat we had been generating started to evidence itself in great streams of perspiration dripping like a faucet without a washer all over their police car, it helped wash the point across. Finally they let us go, but stalked our track the whole way and, at the fifteen minute mark where we turned around and ran back into town, we saw the police cars. One was down the hill behind a trailer park (thinking we couldn't see him) standing by his car under the shade of a tree, watching every move we made. The other was driving by us first one way then the other and keeping tabs on our route.

When we turned a corner to the street where our motel was located, they were there lurking in the shadows. We thought it was rather nice of those gentlemen to give us such careful security and protection.

They would have been a welcome sight a few months later when a car of half drunk teenagers came along in their hot rod one dark night on a lonely road. After roaring by us and shouting crazy remarks, they came down the road again screeching to a stop in front of our path. Three stumbled out and started running with us. The rest of the carload shot off down the road out of sight. What they planned to do we couldn't imagine, but with no houses in sight for a mile or more in this dark night, all kinds of stories ran through our minds about drunk teenagers. Two minutes later the hot rod appeared again, roaring loudly, picking up the drunkest two runners, with the other insisting he could carry on for a little while longer. So they shot off again, and we still had the company of one. As his beer began to give him side aches, he started to slow down amidst grunts and panting breath. Fortunately his friends came back and he crawled into the hot rod.

What amazes me is the length people will go to make fools of themselves. Full-grown people will slow down and shout idiotic, senseless statements, most of which you can't understand, but from the things I can decipher it's not worth understanding.

One night a couple of teenagers who had seen me running before along their street were in their hot rod waiting. As soon as I had gotten a block or so past them, they started down the street and when they were beside me, one of them tossed a bucked of water out of the window. His aim turned out to be rather poor because I ran over it instead of through it.

Many of the truck drivers on the highways who are bored with the thoughts of the long hauls ahead of them are only too ready to play a prank at the first provocation. It was a hot sultry day on the east coast. I was running along a busy highway feeling listless and wilted in the midsummer heat. I had just come down a hill forcing out a slow gait and wondering how I ever got started on this enervating habit, when all at once I heard behind me what sounded like a thousand trumpets blowing right in my ear. No sooner had that died away than I heard a loud boom. Every nerve in my body was jangled completely, and I must have leaped at least three feet into the air. As I came back to my senses, a big semi-trailer truck roared by with the driver bowed over the steering wheel in gales of laughter. The only way I can figure it is that he saw me running as he came over the top of the hill and cut off his motor, coasting down the hill until he got just behind me. As he was tooting the horns he turned the key on, which caused the loud backfire. It seemed to take five years off my life. I was used to having trucks toot, and usually could hear them coming and would make preparation, but when he coasted in behind there was nothing to do but act like a nervous wreck.

Since we had to make the best of wherever we were staying in our travels, we had to solve some pretty involved problems relative to the motoring public who, to say the least, don't give much leeway to hair-brained athletes running through the center of the city, as we sometimes did. Our biggest problem in cities like Miami, New York, and Los Angeles was finding a route that would enable us to avoid the traffic lights, which were always cross roads of congestion.

We executed the maneuver by turning left at the street just before the traffic light, going down one block, then turning right out to the main street, and after turning right again we would pick the opportune moment and get to the other side of the street, and then at the intersection make a left turn again and be back on the same street from which we started.

This worked fine until you got to a section that had a traffic light at every intersection. In that case, and when we happened to strike all the lights red, we would say a prayer take one look, and make a dash for the other side.

Then there is an occurrence that happens quite often, and greatly helps us to pick up speed when energy seems to be hard to come by.

As soon as we make that left turn to get around the traffic light and intersection, we get into the residential districts. Now you yourself know how the American people love dogs, and every home comes equipped with at least one or two. Some Americans take pride in training their dogs to chew on everything that comes within ten feet of their property line. As soon as we turn down these residential streets, the first dog who spots us lets out a howl to warn the rest of his neighborhood militia to stand by for duty.

As we come by each house, they're waiting at the curb and after making a bid for our pant legs and greeting their other cronies by loud barks and growls, they fall in line behind us one by one and amble along, enjoying the leadership and good exercise. All is fine until we reach another main street with cars racing every which way.

As we make a dash to get across the street and beat the traffic, the dogs follow in close formation, but fail to note that we scarcely made it across without being hit by the oncoming cars. As we get to the other side, tons of automobiles descend upon eight unperceiving dogs, and dogs and cars alike scatter in every imaginable direction.

As horns blare, tires squeal, tempers rage, and officers come out of the woodwork, our sneakers quietly carry us around the next corner never to bee seen again.

As soon as we have run fifteen minutes in one direction, we double back and run for the remaining fifteen minutes in the other direction, which takes us back to where we started.

Naturally this type of exercise produces a considerable amount of perspiration, and in order not to evaporate completely, we take a good ice cold shower and drink a good deal of water as soon as we finish.

The type of weather conditions we run in makes a big difference in how much we perspire and accordingly how thirsty we are.

During meetings in Oklahoma City, there was an

unseasonable blizzard and we ran in three inches of snow and naturally heat wasn't as noticeable. The noticeable part about that whole affair was our running attire and quite a sight to behold.

After getting on all the "long johns" we could, we each put on two pairs of heavy pants, two shirts, a sweater, and a heavy overcoat. Then since this was all so unexpected and we had no gloves available, out came wool socks which were used as gloves, then a handkerchief tied over our noses bandit style to keep that section warm, and to top it all off, an aviator hat which covers our ears. Consequently, all that could be seen were two beady eyes peering from between the wrappings and gave the appearance of Arabs on the desert sands. So down the road we ran, fifteen minutes one way and fifteen minutes back, trudging out the miles of exercise and enjoying every minute of it.

In contrast, during an itinerary in the Midwest, it was so hot and we produced so much extra heat while running, it took a good two hours just to get back to where we were dripping wet instead of literal walking faucets.

When Paul and I took up flying, we found it produced a great deal of fatigue. So after coming in from a long flight and flying around the traffic pattern, we would park the airplane and run around the traffic pattern.

Again, let me stress the wonderfully exhilarating experience this is to a person, not only physically but mentally. Many of you business executives, housewives, office workers, and even manual laborers who have your stomach out where you can watch it and a seat to match; if you would just do a little strenuous exercise each day, not running five miles—most of you would keel over dead from heart failure—but start out simply, with determination and a daily plan, it won't be long before that pizza, macaroni, steak, pie, ice cream, candy, and stale fat are all worn away and you'll not only look better but feel better. Your mind also will become alert and alive and mental depression and worry will all but disappear.

The Bible has a lot to say about keeping in good physical condition and you can save a lot of money on doctors, diet books, pills, health clubs, and the like if you just read this book that took 1600 years to write and is a direct work of God through 40 authors.

Elijah, God's prophet, had eaten only two meals a day for forty days in the wilderness, and the Bible records that he kept pace with King Ahab's horses and ran before them to the entrance of Jezreel. (1 Kings 18)

The Apostle Paul walked a great deal, and in Acts 20, when Dr. Luke and the other men took the boat, Paul was "minded to go afoot" and walked from Troas to Assos. He knew what he was talking about when he wrote that bodily exercise is profitable for the little time we are here on earth. He spoke from miles of experience.

After Christ's resurrection, two men are mentioned as walking from Jerusalem to Emmaus (about six miles) talking over the events of Christ's death and "Jesus drew near and went with them." (Luke 24) Yet when it comes to us in this century, we can't even walk to church and back. People are so far from God's plan for good physical health, they run to the doctor every time they get a fever or a cough. And if the baby coughs more than three times in a row they run in frantic desperation to the doctor with, "What's wrong, what's wrong?"

From the time Dad and Ma gave birth to their first son, David, up until the ink went on this paper, nobody, including David, Connie, Arnold III, Elisabeth, Paul, Peter, Timothy, or Charlotte went to the hospital except to be born, and sometimes I wonder if it was even needed then.

Our good health and no-doctor record didn't come about by miracles and wonders, but by good old-fashioned, down to earth common sense. We have absolutely nothing against doctors or the right kind of medicines, but are thankful we have no need of their services. For instance, as soon as Father learned that white sugar was chemically refined and hard on your teeth, we never saw it in the house again. From then on it was either honey, raw, or brown sugar for sweetening.

One day Ma said, "Arnold, this honey and brown sugar is so much more expensive than the good old white sugar, why don't we try to economize and at least get it for cooking and baking?"

Dad replied immediately and resolutely, "Which would you rather do, spend money for doctors and dentists or good wholesome food?"

Mother replied meditatively as she stirred something on the stove, "Well, good wholesome food, I guess."

It wasn't long after that he learned of the process for making white flour, and that the best part of the wheat is separated, and the leftovers bleached, then enriched again (supposedly to bring it back to its former standard of nutrition). All this unnatural way of fooling with God's creation wasn't a bit popular with my father. He said, "God knew what He was doing when he made a wheat kernel and a corn kernel. He didn't intend that they be de-vitalized and de-germinated, then re-vitalized and re-germinated." What capped the climax was learning that they were taking the best part of the wheat and making vitamin pills, then selling the leftovers, bleached and be-draggled as they were, at the regular price in a loaf of bread. He said, "Who wouldn't need vitamin pills after eating that stuff?"

I guess I don't need to tell you that wherever the Pent family set up shop around the country, the dinner table was bare of all processed bread, "alum puff," as Dad used to call it. To show us how puffed up and unhealthy it was, he brought a loaf home and gave a demonstration. "From now on," he said, "we won't be eating this type of bread," and after explaining its evils said, "Now Connie, I want you to set this loaf end up on a chair and sit on it." So Connie did as she was told. When she arose, the family size loaf was equivalent to about three or four regular slices. "See there," said Dad informatively, "this stuff is just what I said it was; 'alum puff.'"

This turn of events was very good for our family for reasons other than health. From then on periodically throughout the month, the unequalled smell of homemade bread, (made with the finest of the wheat and orange blossom honey), would drift lazily through the house and send our appetites into a running fit. It was many an hour that Mother spent (wherever she could get a kitchen) kneading dough and after letting it rise to just the right size, bake it to a golden brown. She was, and is, a wonderful and faithful mother, but somehow when that homemade bread comes out we feel like making her the queen of the earth.

I feel sorry for the children and husbands of these "commercial cake box" mothers who run all over town to their bridge clubs, tea parties, and chit chats, but when it comes to making some good old fashioned homemade bread, they stand there in an expensive dress, fancy shoes, plastered with cosmetics and say, "Oh, my goodness, I just don't have time." Don't they realize that God gave them a family and that faithfulness is the most desired and sought after commodity of this generation? What profit will they see 20 years later as they weep over a delinquent child or an unfaithful husband? (That question doesn't need answering but it does need asking.)

If there was anybody in this world that didn't have time for duties like this, it was my mother. If there was anybody who could have thrown her hands up in despair and said, "I simply cannot do it," it was Mother. She lived out of a suitcase for many months of the year, and many days she did not know where God would put her in the next twenty-four hours.

She didn't have a kitchen to call her own and yet in most places where we would set up for a few days and when things were unsettled, that smell of good old homemade bread from every direction gave us a much needed sense of security no matter how strange the surroundings or difficult the living conditions. Whenever I smell that wonderful identification signal now, I think of the verses in Proverbs describing the virtuous woman.

In the Pent family tradition, the only thing to put on homemade bread is honest-to-goodness real butter. The Bible says, "Butter and honey shall he eat, that he may

know to refuse the evil and choose the good…And it shall come to pass, for the abundance of milk that they shall give he shall eat butter: for butter and honey shall every one eat that is left in the land." I don't know how many times Mother, with economy in mind, would put margarine on the table, trying to get us to eat it, but it was just that many times that somebody around the table would comment about "that slimy axle grease." A case in point was when Dad came in tired and weary from a hard day's work, looking forward to some good homemade bread and butter. With absolutely no intent of malice, Mother put on some margarine of a particularly low pedigree.

We were all sitting around the long dinning room table eating heartily and Mother was looking out of the corner of the eye to see if the margarine could go unnoticed.

Dad was enjoying his meal to the full and really putting it away, when suddenly after taking a bit of bread and "butter," his jaws stopped dead in their tracks, his face set like a Plaster of Paris mold, and his eyes stared with an unfocused glare.

Mother was the first to notice and found it impossible to discourage the sheepish grin that kept forcing its way on

her face. Soon, all eyes were focused on Father's still frame, as his tongue worked itself back and forth on his uppers, trying to get rid of the greasy sensation.

Dad was a long way from smiling when he looked at Mother and said, "Dear, please don't put this stuff on the table again," and with a red face, Mother agreed.

When the nation was told by many so-called experts that butter causes heart trouble and butter fat was clogging people's systems, David informed the whole family one day just before devotions that he believed the reason butter fat was a problem and causing heart trouble was because people nowadays do not get enough physical exercise and the butter, instead of being worked into muscle and energy, clogs the system. "I think," David continued, "we should stay as near as possible to God's natural way of doing things, and real butter is an enjoyable way to do it." Needless to say, there was a hearty "Amen" from every corner of the room. Every corner, that is, except Mother's, who defended, "I can still enjoy a stick of good oleo if there is ever a need for economy." To which David replied, "That's all right except, the best way to really economize is spend the money that profits you the most and eliminate costs that come from living off of food that doesn't feed."

Isaiah also had something to say along this line from Isaiah 55, "Wherefore do ye spend your money for that which is not bread? and your labor for that which satisfieth not? Hearken diligently unto me and eat ye that which is good, and let your soul delight itself in fatness. Incline your ear, and come unto me: hear, and your soul shall live."

If you would like to let other folks support the doctors, just think twice when you go to the grocery store and eat in proportion to your exercise.

We have ten living testimonies that it works.

14

A la Carte

One time we walked aboard a ship from Israel docking in Miami for tourists and cargo. The captain and crew were all natives of Israel and we came with the express purpose of giving them the story of Christ, the Messiah of the Bible.

We climbed the ramp up to the main deck and asked a man for the captain's quarters. He just shrugged his shoulders mumbling something in Hebrew, so we walked on and caught the first stairway up and soon found ourselves at the door of the captain's quarters.

We hadn't been there sixty seconds when a well-dressed Jewish lady approached and informed us that the captain was in the bar with some businessmen from town but she would inform him that we were there.

About three minutes later, he appeared from the lower deck and was a little taken aback that such a crowd was come to see him. Immediately he ushered us into his quarters where he provided chairs for us all and asked why we had come.

Dad didn't answer that question directly yet, but did tell him we were traveling wherever we were invited and encouraging people to come back to God by reading the Bible each day, and we had brought him one to read during his voyages.

After singing "How Great Thou Art" and doing some

more informal chatting he asked what the Bible had to say about ships and the sea, and asked if any one of us could give him one of the stories.

Who could have asked for a better opportunity for Paul to tell him the story of Jonah?

Paul started right in and the man heard, probably for the first time, about a fellow countryman who ran away from God on a ship going to Tarshish, and when God blew up a terrible storm, they threw Jonah overboard and he was swallowed by a great fish; then how Jonah was miraculously vomited up on the shore and decided it was time to obey God and go tell Nineveh to repent of her sins.

Meanwhile, a Jewish couple that had come in with the captain out of curiosity, had about all the religion they could take for the week and said they must leave for a very important appointment, and proceeded to bow out of the room.

As our visit lengthened, the captain grew noticeably nervous and seeing our time was almost up, Father very diplomatically told him that as Jonah was a sign to the Ninevites that they had to repent or perish under God's judgment, so Jesus came and said, "Repent'" and as our Messiah and Savior, laid down his life for our sins and promised to all those who would receive Him as their Lord, everlasting life.

There were twelve of us all together in the room and almost without exception each one had beads of perspiration on his forehead or streams running down his back.

When you talk to people about the eternal well being of their soul and you see they don't want Christ's sacrifice, it not only makes them sweat, but you do your share too. It seems amazing that you can talk all day about what church they go to and kinds of religious activities but when you ask a person about their standing with God, the sweat really starts to roll and in fact most of them see that they also get rolling right away; unless, of course, they are of an honest heart and will receive God's gift of Eternal Life. We parted company with the captain who graciously received the Bible. He said he treasured it and promised to read it.

As we rounded a bend on our way off the ship we unexpectedly ran into the man and wife whom we met in the captain's quarters and who were busily engaged in that important appointment for which they excused themselves. It seems they were standing together busily staring out over the water.

It was a hot Sunday afternoon at the famous Mall in Miami Beach, Florida, and the beach was jammed with people trying to get a tan. As we were led to the spot where we would speak and sing, we could readily see that they weren't exactly the receptive type. We hoped very strongly that they would listen to us and keep quiet, or just mind their own business.

We reached a spot in the middle of the Beach and after a short introduction started singing. You never saw anything the way hundreds of them got up and crowded around us to hear and see this queer bunch of people.

The more we sang the bigger the crowd got, and the bigger the crowd got, the more we sang.

We felt like Shadrach, Meshach, and Abednego in the fiery furnace due to the fact that it was so hot that day and we were in the presence of so many people whose facial expressions and bathing attire didn't exactly denote a life of purity and Godliness. However, we had committed ourselves and there was no turning back now.

It got very quiet as hundreds listened with surprisingly rapt attention. We wanted, if at all possible, to get some good solid Scripture to the crowd without driving them away or losing their attention and Father thought the best way to do that would be to let little Charlotte, then eight years old, be a brave soldier and quote a story from the Old Testament Scriptures. So after a brief introduction by Father of how Charlotte had heard the Bible read every day of her life, she started in on her story of Naaman, the leprous general of the Syrian army, and how God cured him of his leprosy through dipping in the Jordan River seven times. (2 Kings 5)

You could have heard a pin drop as Charlotte practically bowled them all over with her clear enunciation and interesting delivery.

One of the older men standing nearby who had his eyes literally popping out of his head, and mouth wide open with astonishment, suddenly came to his senses and hollered to a man across on the other side, "Hey, Max, give that girl a two year contract." This didn't bother Charlotte in the least for she just kept right on going and as soon as she finished, we followed through with another song.

Twenty minutes had gone by and the crowd kept growing, but it was time to cut it off and go to another section of the beach, so Father, with utmost calmness and confidence told the audience (75% Jewish) that we had put our trust in Jesus Christ who was born of the virgin Mary and after living a life without sin, died on the cross to pay the price that had to be paid for our sins.

He told them that Jesus had now risen from the dead to prove his power to give us Eternal Life and Salvation if we would heed His call when He said, "Come unto me, all ye that labor and are heavy laden, and I will give you rest. Take my yoke upon you, and learn of me; for I am meek and lowly in heart: and ye shall find rest unto your souls. For my yoke is easy, and my burden is light."

Just before we left, we told them that we had available some copies of the New Testament, and if there were some who sincerely wanted them and would promise to read them, they could have them free of charge.

As soon as the meeting broke up, we were almost mobbed by hands reaching for the New Testament and they not only took every Testament, but every last piece of literature brought for the occasion, some even offering money to pay the cost.

As we began to get older and our singing improved to the point we were carrying four-part harmony and making many of our own arrangements, many people suggested that we get on television.

Several times as we went into large cities, we would be guests of not one T.V. channel, but all the channels in the city.

One by one they would invite us to come to one of their programs and would give us anywhere from three minutes to thirty minutes free of charge.

One time while in one of the leading cities of the south, we were invited to share a half hour Sunday morning T.V. program with one of the local churches. Everybody that was to be on the program was at the studio for final rehearsal forty-five minutes before the videotape was to be made. The rehearsal went just as planned and it looked like everything would dovetail perfectly.

As a matter of fact, all did go well, except for one highly embarrassing moment for our mixed quartet number.

Before the video tape started rolling, we had everything to the point of absolute perfection, including how to walk out on the set in front of the cameras where our guitar amplifier was to be located for the best balance with the singing, and what to do when we finished our number.

Our electric guitars had to have one wire going from

the guitar into the amplifier and the wires were about five feet in length.

Everyone was a little tense as the preacher finished his announcements, and all the lights went on where Connie, Paul, Elisabeth, and I were to walk out with the camera following us.

All was perfect silence as the producer signaled to our mixed quartet to walk on the set and sing. We were on T.V.!

I was first in line and confidently stepped into the bright lights with the others following close behind.

To our eternal embarrassment, one of the sound technicians had unknowingly moved our guitar amplifier back two feet, leaving our allowable distance to walk on the set only about three feet instead of the five I had been calculating, due to the length of our cords. As I confidently strode on the set with head erect and shoulders back (before an audience of half a million people) I was suddenly jerked to a dead stop and swung around like the crack of a whip and stood facing those staring cameras. Meanwhile, Connie, who was next in line behind me, before the "go" signal was given, got tangled up in my guitar cords and was straddling it with one foot on one side and one foot on the other.

When she took the first step, she knew what the trouble was without looking and started taking high prancing steps like a thoroughbred walking horse trying to get on one side of the cord or the other. But alas, as I came to a premature stop she not only remained neatly tangled, but bumped into me as well.

Fortunately for Connie, but unfortunately for the audience, who must have been having fun watching our faces turn crimson with embarrassment, we did not have to walk off the set while the cameras were watching.

170

Incidentally, this was color T.V.!

We were always excited about being on T.V. because it gave such opportunity to reach so many, and without fail, increased our attendance at public meetings.

One time in Miami, Florida, when making our first recording for public release, we were invited by the local station, owned and managed by Jewish people, to give a program. They received so many phone calls afterward that we were invited back two more times, and as a result, the competing channel who saw the programs invited us over for a complete thirty minute program Sunday morning.

Father was born to be a salesman. One time in another city he decided to just go right into the office and sell the program manager on the idea of having us on his station.

He told us all to get dressed in our best bib and tucker and be ready for anything as he introduced us to the man with whom he had made the appointment.

This was our first experience with T.V. and we were all nervous wrecks as we walked into the studio.

However, not one of us could anywhere near match the nervousness of Mother at these times. Being of a quiet nature and not aggressive along these lines, these were times when she did some soul-searching and wondered why in the world she got into this mess and why she married this man and had all these children; when instead she could have easily gotten a financially successful gentleman from the Boston area where she was reared, and could have lived in peaceful tranquility. (The tranquility might have been peaceful but my guess is that it would also have been unproductive. Proverbs 14:4 says, "Where no oxen are, the crib is clean: but much increase is by the strength of the ox," and if things are going to be accomplished, somebody has to pitch in and do the dirty

171

work which many times grates against one's inherited nature. Of course she realized this and courageously braved the storm the best she knew how.)

Twenty minutes after walking into the studio "cold turkey" we were singing the diadem tune of "All Hail the Power of Jesus Name" with all our might on the popular noon day program. For fifteen minutes thereafter, we worked hard on the theme of encouraging families to read the Bible and give their lives to Christ. Since it wasn't in order to do much actual preaching, Father had the whole family stand together and recite verses from the Bible on the theme of Salvation.

As David gave a reference such as John 3:16, we would all thunder together to an audience of a million people, "For God so loved the world, that he gave his only begotten Son, that whosoever believeth in him should not perish, but have everlasting life." Then he would give the next reference: "John 5:24," and all ten strong, we would enthusiastically tell them, "Verily, verily, I say unto you, He that heareth my word, and believeth on him that sent me, hath everlasting life, and shall not come into condemnation; but is passed from death unto life."

When we were on television in Los Angeles, it was an all night telethon that went from 12 o'clock Saturday night until 9 o'clock Sunday morning. We were on three times during the night and the remainder of the time helped answer the telephones in the studio where hundreds of people called during the night. The number was flashed on the screen every half hour and people with all types of problems and in all kinds of trouble would call and ask question on how their lives could be straightened out. Many would ask us how we managed to work together so well and we would simply tell them, "We just read the

Bible every day and ask God to help us and it works."
Many of them tried it and found that, yes, it does work.

Driving through Los Angeles the next year, a man
came out of the blue, stopped us right in traffic and
hollering through the car window said, "I saw you last year
on television and it was great," then sped off again.

Connie compiled a list of reasons to read the Bible
every day. These would apply to all of us.

1. The Lord commands it. "Meditate upon these things;
give thyself wholly to them; that thy profiting may appear
to all. Take heed unto thyself, and unto the doctrine;
continue in them: for in doing this thou shalt both save
thyself, and them that hear thee." 1 Timothy 4:15,16

2. I want to be fruitful. "Abide in me, and I in you. As
the branch cannot bear fruit of itself, except it abide in the
vine; no more can ye, except ye abide in me. I am the vine,
ye are the branches: He that abideth in me, and I in him,
the same bringeth forth much fruit: for without me ye can
do nothing." John 15:4,5

3. I want to know true doctrine. "Then said Jesus to
those Jews which believed on him, If ye continue in my
word, then are ye my disciples indeed; And ye shall know
the truth, and the truth shall make you free." John 8:31,32

4. I want to be clean. "Now ye are clean through the
word which I have spoken unto you." John 15:3

5. I want my prayers answered. "If ye abide in me, and
my words abide in you, ye shall ask what ye will, and it
shall be done unto you." John 15:7

6. I want to be prosperous and successful. "This book of
the law shall not depart out of thy mouth; but thou shalt
meditate therein day and night, that thou mayest observe
to do according to all that is written therein: for then thou
shalt make thy way prosperous, and then thou shalt have

good success." Joshua 1:8

7. I don't want to backslide. "The law of his God is in his heart; none of his steps shall slide." Psalm 37:31

8. I want my soul fed. "And he humbled thee, and suffered thee to hunger, and fed thee with manna, which thou knewest not, neither did thy fathers know; that he might make thee know that man doth not live by bread only, but by every word that proceedeth out of the mouth of the Lord doth man live." Deuteronomy 8:3

9. I want to grow. "As newborn babes, desire the sincere milk of the word, that ye may grow thereby." 1 Peter 2:2

10. I want understanding. "I have more understanding than all my teachers: for thy testimonies are my meditation." Psalm 119:99

11. I want real life. "It is the spirit that quickeneth; the flesh profiteth nothing: the words that I speak unto you, they are spirit, and they are life." John 6:63

12. I want to be thoroughly furnished to every good work. "All scripture is given by inspiration of God, and is profitable for doctrine, for reproof, for correction, for instruction in righteousness: That the man of God may be perfect, thoroughly furnished unto all good works." 2 Timothy 3:16,17

15

Influencing Children

The trouble today perhaps is not so much with delinquent children, but delinquent parents. In the first place, the fathers are not obeying the Lord, then the mothers are not obeying their husbands as God commands in Ephesians 5:24 and 1 Peter 3:1-6, and with these irregularities, how can the children ever learn to obey their parents? Children are not as likely to be obedient when their spiritual lives are warped from the lack of nourishment in the Word of God. Jeremiah said, "Thy words were found and I did eat them, and thy word was unto me the Joy and rejoicing of my heart." Children must, they just must, have a daily diet of the Word of God! If they do not, they immediately adjust their eyesight and insight on the material things of life and that outlook alone will never make good children, good citizens, or good parents in years to come. And incidentally, a little devotional each morning is not enough. The Bible has to be read by chapters and books. We go through the Bible 8 to 10 times a year including family and private devotions and we've got a long way to go to be perfect. The truth is, the more we read the Bible, the more we see how undeserving we are of God's grace.

The second reason children are not obedient is because

their parents do not require it. The Lord said, "train up a child," "Thou shalt teach these things diligently to thy children," and "A child left to himself bringeth his mother to shame."

I remember being entertained in a minister's home in Western New York where we were having meetings. Though Paul and I then fifteen and eighteen years, stayed there for three days, we scarcely saw the minister's sixteen-year-old son. One night we came in from a meeting and I said to the minister, "Where is your son? I'd like to get to know him a little better."

"Oh," he said, waving his hand with a carefree motion. "I don't know. He just said he was going out and would be back about midnight."

When I was sixteen, my father knew everywhere I went and required me to be home at a specific time. Everybody else in our family was treated the same way. Sixteen years old is a crucial time in anybody's life, whether they realize it or not, and happy is the young person who has parents smart enough to plan character building activities and require respect and obedience.

As we have traveled across the country, I have beheld the sad misery of families whose parents required religion but didn't teach Christ and tried to get their children to like the church without ever bothering to spend daily time in the Word of God around a family alter.

First of all, a dead religion without a personal relationship with Jesus Christ is hopeless enough, but when it is forced on a child and appears to be the only thing that this world has to offer for moral upbuilding and true personality development, it doesn't generate much enthusiasm on the part of a young person.

Solomon said, "He has made everything beautiful in His time" and there is nothing more beautiful than to see a child quietly listening to the profound wisdom God has set down in His Word. He may not understand it all, for that takes much time, but he can learn much more than many of us think. Psalm 119:99 says, "I have more understanding than all my teachers, for thy testimonies are my meditation." If we want strong leaders, not only in our churches, but in business and government, the father and mother must take time out of their busy schedule of church work, social life, business, and housework to sit quietly with the whole family and read the Bible.

The third reason children do not obey their parents is because parents allow them to be subjected to influences that teach lawlessness and disobedience and lack of trust in God.

The main reason Father took us out of school was due to a trend that has now fully developed into outright godlessness. He saw our behavior, in spite of the family devotions, become increasingly rowdy and unruly. He and Mother felt that a majority of our day should not be spent in that atmosphere; God has honored that decision and enabled Father and Mother, working together, to do something which seems an impossibility in the eyes of men—educating eight children from kindergarten to college.

16

Gold Rush Country

In the horse and buggy days, many preachers set
out on the weekends in the old buckboard to preach the
Gospel in the towns, villages, and countryside that had no
witness for Jesus Christ. After preaching many times and
suffering untold privations and hardships, they bounced
home to start another week of plowing or watching sheep.

In this "enlightened" age (and spiritually dead), many
preachers won't even open their mouths unless the church
provides a beautiful home and a bountiful salary. When the
church board does agree to terms, in many cases the pastor
has to make some concessions or compromises to keep
the salary payers happy. If you wonder why you don't hear
much about "sin, righteousness, and judgment to come"
in your pulpit today, just check the financial set-up and
see how "the just shall live by faith"-faith in the budget,
faith in the members, faith in fellow men. What about
faith in God? I'm not saying preachers should not be paid.
The Bible says, "Let the elders that rule well be counted
worthy of double honor, especially they who labor in the
word and doctrine. For the Scripture saith, Thou shalt not
muzzle the ox that treadeth out the corn. And, The laborer
is worthy of his reward." (I Timothy 5:17-18) Preachers
should be the best paid of anybody, but only when they

179

preach the Gospel of Christ in power and simplicity!

Jeremiah said, "Woe be unto the pastors that destroy and scatter the sheep of my pasture! saith the Lord. Behold, I am against the prophets, saith the Lord, that use their tongues, and say, He saith. Behold, I am against them that prophesy false dreams, saith the Lord, and do tell them, and cause my people to err by their lies, and by their lightness; yet I sent them not, nor commanded them: therefore they shall not profit this people at all, saith the Lord." (Jeremiah 23:1, 31-32)

I have never ceased to marvel at the simplicity that Father uses in his preaching. Sometimes I wonder why he keeps it so simple and yet it cannot be denied that God by His Spirit has done a great work in the lives that heard it.

Well, we were off on another trip and only the Lord knew how long it was going to be and where we would end up. The only direct invitation was from the Northern California mining section of Sutter's Mill where the gold was first discovered that started the great California gold rush in the 1880s.

When we arrived, the gold was gone, but people were still there trying to make a living off the land. There was a great need in the whole area for a witness to the saving and keeping power of Jesus Christ.

As in so many cases, we arrived with absolutely no money and no invitation to be there. And as in so many cases, our faith began to wear thin with the thought that nobody cared where we were and wouldn't have cared if they did know.

There also, as in so many cases, Father spoke during breakfast devotions this first morning we arrived; "We know that the Lord has sent us here for some purpose and we need to ask Him to make clear to us what his perfect will is. He promises, 'The meek will he guide in judgment:

and the meek will he teach his way!' (Psalm 25:9) Connie, I'll ask you to pray now and ask the Lord to make us meek and submissive to His perfect will and use us for the Glory of God in this lonely country."

Our first devotion time was conducted in a little rough hewn log cabin that a Christian lady said we could use during our stay if we would be able to clean out all the old junk that had accumulated there over the years.

When our half-hour of Bible reading was over, Mother said, "Who will volunteer to get this place cleaned up and fit for human beings?"

So Connie, Elisabeth, and Peter started to work, carrying out old feed bags, stove pipes, cans, glass bottles, etc. and swept everything clean (at least as clean as a dirt floor can be).

By afternoon the preacher, a few country blocks away, offered an extra room for any of us boys that would like to stay there, saying that snow was very likely to fall that night and we might be more comfortable.

The next morning as we gathered for a conference, blond, blue-eyed Timothy stood up to all of us confidently and said, "Last night we could see the stars through our roof and this morning when I woke up snow was coming in the cracks."

The next day we received an invitation by phone from a lumber camp way back off the beaten track requesting us to put on a program. The message went through several hands before reaching us, but when it finally did arrive, Father gave the O.K. for an appearance at the end of the week.

The roads turned out to be nothing but gravel, and a bad drought going on at the time helped to make it a long, dusty miserable ride over back mountain trails.

As our two cars drove into the camp, a welcoming committee was waiting to greet us. Mother stepped wearily from the car and greeted the folks that had come out.

A rather well built lady, who had been nice enough to prepare a meal for us, stepped forward from the group and welcomed Mother, but a look of surprise coupled with a hint of disillusionment came over her as she saw us all gathering around.

"Oh my goodness," she said, "I was told that you were a family of fourteen black children."

We never did find out who got the message mixed up nor have we run across the black family with fourteen children. It is interesting to see what can happen when a message is relayed by telephone into the back woods, especially when

the folks have the exclusiveness of a fifteen party line.

After enjoying a good supper and chatting amiably with the few Christians that lived in the camp, the meeting, packed with tough men and boys from all over the face of this earth, got under way. Many of them were outcasts of society and had come here trying to earn money, and others were just ungodly men with an independent and adventuresome spirit. Most had come to the meeting just because there was nothing else to do and out of curiosity.

Father started the program with a word of introduction and as he talked, we all grouped around him for the first song together, which was "How Great Thou Art."

What amazed me then, and still does, was the change of appearance on those tough unforgiving faces as I glanced around the audience. Men who had lived in sin and darkness all their lives and probably never heard the gospel clearly presented sat with earnest and hungry eyes portraying the hopelessness of their lost condition before God. We watched them as they started to realize that "Jesus Christ came into the world to save sinners" and would actually save them.

After the message, twenty-five lumbermen professed Jesus Christ as their Savior and confessed openly that they now believed.

The Word of God had done its work again and lives had been changed. I thought of the verse in Jeremiah 23:29, "Is not my word like as a fire? saith the Lord; and like a hammer that breaketh the rock in pieces?"

After giving our testimony as a family all over that gold rush countryside, Father got a postcard from a layman in Redding, California asking us to come there and give our testimony in the churches.

I'll never forget the night we arrived. It was just about dusk and slow drizzle gave off just enough moisture in the air to make us sticky and easily annoyed.

The total financial assets didn't help cheer anybody up either. I think Father had about thirteen dollars in his pocket. After registering at the most inexpensive motel in town, the assets went to four dollars.

"Now," said Father, matter-of-factly, "All I could get was

one double bed, so we'll have to all do the best we can in fixing up a place for everybody to lie down. Peter and Timothy, get the night bags in and then we'll have evening devotions."

By the time all ten had gotten in and the night bags and suitcases had arrived, there was about as much sleeping room as in a space capsule.

For devotions that night we were reading in the Minor Prophets, and David brought Haggai 1:6 -7 to our attention as we read through that book.

"Ye have sown much, and bring in little; ye eat, but ye have not enough; ye drink, but ye are not filled with drink; ye clothe you, but there is none warm; and he that earneth wages earneth wages to put it into a bag with holes." "We can thank the Lord," said Dave triumphantly as he sat on the floor over in the corner, "that even though we're so low on money most of the time and sometimes barely seem to make it, we are sowing the incorruptible seed of the Word of God. It always brings in a harvest and instead of putting our money into a bag with holes, we are laying up treasure in Heaven with what little we can get, and it will never be lost."

The next morning, Mother suggested that we check out of the motel after Father had phoned the man who had written the card and invited us here. We were scheduled to meet with him and another man at the Post Office at 11 A.M.

Our two cars were parked in front of the Post Office ten minutes earlier than the time appointed. Father has always taught us that the early bird catches the worm and practiced what he preached.

Unfortunately, we were not too well dressed or pressed at the time because of two days of traveling, but everybody fixed up as best they could.

Father had gone into the Post Office to mail some

letters and as the heat of the day grew, Peter, Timothy, and
Charlotte (then 8, 5, & 3 years old), began to fuss and
fume over the crowded condition in the car.

Just then a very well dressed and important looking
man came to Mother's window and said, "You're not part
of the Pent Family are you?"

Mother was somewhat taken back at first, but regained
her composure and said with her typical Boston accent and
nervous smile, "Why, yes we are."

"Well, " said the man cheerily, "I was told you would
be here and just wanted to make your acquaintance and
learn more about the wonderful job you are doing. I
don't know how you do it! It just seems like a physical
impossibility." Mother, wondering at that moment how she
did it herself, expressed an answer in conservative Boston
style, "Well, the Lord gives us enough strength to live a day
at a time and that's all we need."

"Where are you folks staying while you're here?" he
asked with concern.

If you want to meet somebody with a conscience that's
so clear you can see through it, then you should meet
Mother, because when it comes to questions like the one
asked, she tells all and never will try to make anybody
think any differently than the perfect truth. With her eyes
dancing from parking meter to parking meter and letting
a little embarrassment sneak in she said, "Right now we're
staying in the city park."

This is not what you would consider a promotional
statement by any stretch of the imagination, but like I said,
that's the way Mother is.

"Oh, I see," he said thoughtfully. "I'll tell you what,
why don't you folks just plan on staying with us tonight."

As Mother thought of the four dollars left in Dad's

packet, it sounded like a capital idea and when he came back from mailing the letters, it was agreed that the whole Pent family would be over at 5 P.M. to the businessman's house. "Well, I'd better be going. I've got to get right home and tell my wife that we're feeding and sleeping ten people tonight." After spending not one, but two nights with this hospitable Christian man and his family, phone calls came inviting us to present programs in many churches and clubs all over the area. This is always most gratifying, especially when you come into a city unknown and unannounced and feel like a regular oddball for doing things so differently. But the Lord says, "Them that honor me, I will honor" and the Lord knew our motives and gave us many opportunities to spread the Gospel.

Later, one particularly comforting phone call for Mother came and offered a completely furnished house for as long as we needed it. Not only that, they said the refrigerator and freezer were full and to use everything we needed. You can imagine what a boost that was to the morale.

I thought of the promise God gives us in Deuteronomy 6:11, "And houses full of all good things, which thou fillest not, and wells digged, which thou diggest not, vineyards and olive trees, which thou plantest not."

17

An Average Day

An average day for our family is not very average to most of the world. Trying to give you a description of an average day is almost impossible because each day we are presented with such new and diversified situations. However, though our activities are varied, there are two things which we do every day without fail, no matter what comes, or what our schedule happens to be, or what the cost.

The first and most important thing we have always done is have family devotions, which has included reading the Bible, singing, and praying. The Bible says, "The law of his God is in his heart; none of his steps shall slide." (Psalm 37:31) It also says that we are to meditate upon these things and give ourselves wholly to them. Why then would we try to take shortcuts to spirituality by cheating our families and ourselves and ignoring the Bible, prayer, and work for God?

You and your children may be making good money, providing for the family, and enjoying a good social standing in the community. If you profess to be a Christian and you accomplish only this, you are like clouds without water and wind without rain when it comes to giving the world a witness of Christ-or even your neighbor. The Bible still says, "What shall it profit a man if he gain the whole world and lose his own life?" A life that is not invested for the glory of Christ is profitless and a dismal failure. It is a life that loses its golden opportunity to spend recklessly the unlimited treasures of God's love, hope, and grace, "In whom are hid all the treasures of wisdom and knowledge." (Colossians 2:3)

During our inevitable occasions of rebellion and obstreperous behavior in regard to devotions, we would hear Dad quoting to us loud and clear from the Bible, "Meditate upon these things; give thyself wholly to them; that thy profiting may appear to all. Take heed unto thyself, and unto the doctrine; continue in them: for in doing this thou shalt both save thyself, and them that hear thee."

The prerequisite for getting a good start every morning is getting to bed on time so that you can get up on time, well rested and ready to go. Ever since Dad came out of college, he has followed a rigid discipline of moderate eating, sufficient sleep, and plenty of exercise. Then, being of the strong conviction and having something good to pass on to others, he diligently trained us to live the same way. Rarely did we ever get to bed after 10 p.m. and most of the time 9:30 found the lights out, and woe to anybody who tried to do otherwise without permission.

So, after a good night's sleep, an average day for our family started with a morning devotional. However, it was so far from most people's concept of a devotional that you will probably have some other name for it. The typical 20th century "Family Altar" is where the father pulls out a devotional booklet, reads a couple of verses to his family before breakfast, or maybe in the evening, then says a prayer. He barely has time to get to the "Amen" when everybody is halfway out the door on his or her way to the day's activities.

As soon as we reached reading age, Father instructed us

to get up before breakfast and have at least fifteen minutes of Bible reading quietly to ourselves. Then he would add dryly, "You can have more time reading the Bible if you want to, but it has to be at least fifteen minutes." It might be noted right here that if we read over the required fifteen minutes, it was purely by accident; at that age and that time of day (early morning) we weren't too enthusiastically cooperative.

Father always practiced what he preached, but hardly a day went by when he didn't preach to us what he practiced. Due to his determination and daily reading, we were convinced that this habit of daily Bible reading, if followed, would go a long way in bringing about solutions to the myriad of problems that the world faces today. And also due to his determination and guidance, by the time we were eighteen years old we were not only practicing what he preached but also preaching to others what we ourselves now practiced.

In spite of ourselves, it turned out to be easier than we thought, and much was learned during these formative years. However, this isn't the end of the story as far as devotions go; we're just beginning.

At the age of nine, our time was increased to thirty minutes before breakfast. By thirteen, at least an hour was required of Bible reading before breakfast.

Trying to read anything for a whole hour before breakfast can be a very trying affair if you don't get to bed on time and must miss sleep to keep on schedule and still get this time in. As you sit there trying to read, your eyes fall shut with your head nodding back and forth, making concentration useless, and also making the practice equally so. Therefore, you can understand why we were trained to go to bed on time.

As a matter of fact, even when you do get to bed on time and get eight hours of sleep, trying to read a whole hour before breakfast still requires self discipline, but the dividends are so great that it is worth every minute spent. Not only do you feed your soul on the Bread of Life, but also if you look at it from a purely educational standpoint, Emily Post has said, "If you want to speak good English, just read the King James Version of the Bible." Martin Luther also said, "Scripture without comment is the sun whence all teachers receive their light." One of the past presidents of Yale University was once asked, "If you had your choice, which would you choose first, a college education or a knowledge of the Bible? He replied without a moment's hesitation, "A knowledge of the Bible."

The fact that we sometimes had some difficulty keeping our eyes open during the early morning reading brought on a new rule from Dad which at its beginning brought some healthy whining and under-the-breath mutterings from all of us at one time or another. The new rule was that everybody had to have a tall glass of water before reading.

At first it seemed almost impossible to get that stuff down early in the morning and all must confess they had their cheating moments when, although the glass itself was tall which they were drinking from, that was where the tallness ended. The water certainly didn't come very high in the glass. However, surprisingly enough, after we acquired the habit, it seemed quite natural to do it. In fact, sometimes we would even be thirsty. However, that was rare. A few more months passed and we were recommending this habit to other people, telling them that it cured chronic headaches, kept away colds, and generally kept you toned up. One thing it really does better than anything else, it brings you to your senses immediately and cuts out this stumbling around the house the first hour of the day. Try it! Especially try the Bible reading.

Spend a certain amount of time alone with God and your life will be much richer for it. It gives you a good start for the day, and we know by experience that for the time you invest, God will enable you to accomplish much more in the Spiritual realm and even to make gains physically and financially. "They that seek the Lord shall not want any good thing." (Psalm 34:10).

David said in Psalms, "Thou through thy commandments hast made me wiser than mine enemies: for they are ever with me. I have more understanding than all my teachers: for thy testimonies are my meditation." (Psalm 119:98,99)

Incidentally, now that your wheels are turning and you are wondering how much you yourself should read the Bible every day, we'll finish telling about our schedule for an average day.

After breakfast, nobody left the house until we had half an hour of devotions as a family. The devotions before breakfast were private devotions, but this was for everybody, reading, praying, and singing together.

Sometimes things got a little sluggish, and it was hard to get everybody together and quiet for reading. So Dad, who has great faith in the effectiveness of rewards, would holler through the house, "The first one to read in the regular place is free from all duties." This of course made a mad scramble and devotions were started immediately.

Then there were times when he would reverse the tactics and instead of rewards to get the devotions going, he would offer punishments. In that case you would hear the walls echoing this familiar refrain, "The last one in here seated with a Bible in his hand will wash the breakfast dishes." If he were particularly riled with our slowness, he would make the punishment stiffer, to the tune of, "The last one here will wash, dry, clear, and put away all the dishes for one week."

Though this statement wasn't enforced too often,
it did pack a real punch, and the thought of having to
wash dishes for ten people, three meals a day, really sent
everybody scampering.

With the whole family seated and doing nothing but
listening we would read. But it wasn't Dad or Ma piously
opening the Bible and reading eight or ten verses. No sir!
We started with David, the oldest, and went right down
the line by age with everybody reading a whole chapter.

As you can see, Dad didn't take the Bible lightly, and
as we came along and realized he meant business, we all
settled down to listening. He knew it was God's Word and
unerring in fact. He was willing to give up anything and
everything (and he did give up a lot) to see that we received
this great heritage.

When we complained about the devotions being too
long, he didn't argue; he just quoted the Bible, "Faith
cometh by hearing the Word of God"; "These words shall
be in thine heart and thou shalt teach them diligently to
thy children", etc.

He told us we should feed our souls as much as we did
our bodies. Since our souls are more important and needed
to be strengthened daily, we had half an hour of devotions
after each meal.

We would read the Old Testament in the morning
after breakfast. Then at noon we read the New Testament,
and at night after supper it was the Old Testament again.

Alternating like this between the Old and New helped
keep our interest up, especially when we got to places like
Leviticus or Numbers where the Bible goes into such detail
about how the Children of Israel sacrificed animals for their
sins or where it describes the building of the Tabernacle.
Many of these chapters to us were just downright boring,

and the method of alternating was very helpful. However, although these certain chapters were boring at the time, and it seemed such a waste of time to hear them, as we got older we began to understand the great truths contained in each one. Had it not been for the fact that we heard them read in our early youth, we would not even have begun to understand them until much later in life.

If you really train up a child in the way he should go, when he is old he will not depart from it, but it seems that most people lack the faith and love for the Lord to dedicate their time to the training of their children. Instead of real spiritual training, they depend on a devotional booklet and Sunday School to magically make them spiritual giants.

Sacrifices must be made if children are to understand doctrine; but actually, it really isn't a sacrifice at all when you look at it over a period of time. If they are trained in God's way, they will not only take care of you in your old age, but also will lead useful lives and be the most valuable people in the community.

Peter, who is the sixth child down the line, started spending his time during early morning Bible reading in the Psalms. For some reason the short Psalms of degrees were appealing to him, (Psalm 120-134, called "Songs of Degree" were chanted by the Children of Israel as they walked up the steps of the Temple for sacrifices). In a few months, he began quoting them during devotions and at the age of ten, he knew each one perfectly and could quote them in public.

I learned to quote the story of David and Goliath and the book of Second Timothy the same way and at about the same age. And each one as they came along around ten years old could easily quote over 300 verses and very little time was spent memorizing.

During our family devotions, Father would always

make sure that nothing else was being done except listening. Ma loved to do the dishes during this time, but Father cured her of that. All of us at one time or another tried getting various things done during devotions so we could kill two birds with one stone, but we were always caught by Father's diligent lookout, and usually he plunked us down and told us to read two chapters instead of one.

In learning the English language, you find there are exceptions to every rule. Here, also, there were exceptions to the rule of absolute stillness during reading.

Sometimes during the week and especially on weekends, churches and schools called upon us to present our programs of music and Scripture presentations. Sometimes it necessitated a long driving time from our motel or house or wherever we were and there just wasn't time to eat, get dressed and loaded, and have devotions in the usual manner. So the loudest reader, like Paul or David, would sit in a central location and read the Bible as we got dressed and ready. If somebody's turn came and they weren't ready to read, they would quote a chapter at the top of their lungs so that each one could hear.

Sometimes being pressed for time, we would have the half hour devotions in our cars as we drove. This necessitated a little extra work because bouncing along the road was not conducive to good reading and since we had to divide into two cars, it was necessary for each one to quote about three chapters or more to fill up the time.

One time, an old friend stopped by to visit whom we hadn't seen for quite some time. We were just finishing dinner. After talking a while, Dad said enthusiastically, "We were just going to do some Bible reading. Would you like to join us?" Much to our surprise, he all of a sudden had to be somewhere for some previous engagement and disappeared into thin air.

Later that week, another friend came by at about the same time of day. After talking half an hour about nothing in particular and everything in general, Dad surmised that he didn't have anything special to do and invited him to stay for reading.

It's hard to believe, but in thirty seconds he had thought of so many things to do you would have thought he was the manager of General Motors.

After a few more experiences like that, we realized how little desire and appreciation people have for the Bible, mostly because they have not been taught early in life of its value in everyday living.

As the years went by, we traveled longer and farther throughout the continent and our programs became more in demand. We were having an average of one or two meetings a day for months at a time. This meant we had to streamline everything we did so as to get everything done that ordinarily had to be done, plus practice our new songs and programs, etc. for the itinerary of meetings.

During our stops, it was rough while staying in people's houses to get in these times of devotion. People would constantly be talking about arrangements being made for sleeping, eating, traveling, etc., plus the never-ending presence of people wanting to visit and ask questions about our travels.

Many times there was much more noise than Father desired, and he would get everybody's attention and say, "We'll be having some Bible reading here for a while and we'd be glad to have you folks join us if you like." As soon as he said that, the multitudes began to melt away and disappear into the woodwork, and Father had his desired peace and quiet.

When the Children of Israel were just about to enter the promised land, the Lord told Joshua, "This book of the law shall not depart out of thy mouth; but thou shalt meditate therein day and night, that thou mayest observe to do according to all that is written therein: for then thou shalt make thy way prosperous, and then thou shalt have good success." Success is what we all want, isn't it?

My mother has often said, "During the time when the children were all much younger and going through rebellious stages of one kind and another, it just didn't seem we were making progress with all the Bible reading we did. But as the months and years went by, and they started becoming conscious of the world around them, I saw that spiritual seed coming to life and giving an unending stream of Godly insight and a desire and determination to spend their lives for Christ."

There has been unending fruit from this practice of reading the Bible daily. This one routine has transformed our family and thousands of others' more than any good book or good habit or self-help formula. God's promises are true.

The second thing our family practiced daily which made our not very average day far more stable and orderly than the average day for an average family, is found in Ephesians 5:22-24: "Wives, submit yourselves unto your own husbands, as unto the Lord. For the husband is the head of the wife, even as Christ is the head of the church: and he is the savior of the body. Therefore as the church is subject unto Christ, so let the wives be to their own husbands in everything."

Very soon after my mother was married to my father, she learned, with a few reminders from Dad, that those verses mean what they say and that even though very few people heed them, she was going to. Mother received the instruction of the Bible and obeyed her husband. In doing so, she discovered that following this Bible passage

196

set the tone for peace and order and unity within the
whole family. Now she recommends that all women do
the same insofar as the husband's orders do not conflict
with what the Bible teaches. This is the only way good
order and proper authority can be handled, and it certainly
produces better and more stable homes both for parents
and children. It is not an insult for women to be in
subjection to their husbands for that is God's order of
life. The woman who does it will find peace, security, and
fulfillment of her desires.

Of course, the husband must also fulfill his God given
responsibility not only in giving directions, but also doing it
in love and according to God's will. The Bible plainly states,
"Husbands, love your wives, even as Christ also loved the
church, and gave himself for it;" and also, "Nevertheless let
everyone of you in particular so love his wife even as himself;
and the wife see that she reverence her husband."

You will never find anything anywhere in the Bible
that teaches a fifty-fifty marriage. That worldly philosophy,
in fact, leads to families falling apart. God's system works.
When families follow His plan for the family, each individual
is protected and benefited. God's system is that the husband
follows God, the wife follows the husband, and the children
follow the parents. Then there is order, peace, and joy.

Roger Babson, the great statistician, has said,
"Children are the best investment you can have." This
is absolutely true, provided they are reared in the fear of
God. Otherwise, you have wasted your time, energy, and
money because if they are not, they usually turn out to be
monsters instead of men.

My mother often says that when she was a girl, her
mother impressed her with the verse in First Timothy
5:14, "I will therefore that the younger women marry,

bear children, guide the house, give none occasion to the adversary to speak reproachfully." Due to the eight results (us children), I'm rather inclined to believe that her mother really drove that verse home.

An average day for our family may not look like an average day for your family. But what is true for all of us is the necessity of infusing into our lives Bible reading as a family and individually throughout the day and following God's order of authority. This direction within the family gives our day, average or not, the right foundation. Then, no matter what else the Lord has given us to do, it will be profitable and truly successful.

Pent Family Photos

LEFT TO RIGHT: *Dr. Pent, Mrs. Pent, Peter, Timothy, Arnold III, Charlotte, Connie, Paul, Elizabeth, and David*

World's Most Unusual Family—Record Album

The Dr. Arnold Pent Family—Record Album

The Homestead College of Bible and Graduate School

From its incorporation in 1964 and the securing of its charter with the State, over forty years of Bible education have continued unabated, now under the Presidency of the eldest son, Dr. David Arnold Pent. Its motto—"The Bible, the whole Bible, and nothing but the Bible"—defines both its method and system, together with its supreme objective of conveying the richest possible knowledge of the Word of God to its students and candidates.

For a free brochure providing College information or a copy of the booklet *An Earnest Contention for the Faith*, which describes further historical developments, write:

The Homestead College of Bible
P.O. Box 1
Orlando, Florida 32802-0001

or visit our Web site: www.collegeofbible.homestead.com